# CAREERS
## IN FOREIGN LANGUAGES

# VGM Professional Careers Series

# CAREERS
## IN FOREIGN LANGUAGES

## BLYTHE CAMENSON

*VGM Career Books*

Chicago   New York   San Francisco   Lisbon   London   Madrid   Mexico City
Milan   New Delhi   San Juan   Seoul   Singapore   Sydney   Toronto

**Library of Congress Cataloging-in-Publication Data**

Camenson, Blythe.
    Careers in foreign languages / Blythe Camenson.
        p.    cm. — (VGM professional careers series)
    Includes bibliographical references.
    ISBN 0-658-00110-8 — ISBN 0-658-00111-6 (pbk.)
    1. Language and languages—Vocational guidance.   I. Title.   II. Series.

P60 .C36   2001
418'0023—dc21

00-69325

# VGM Career Books

*A Division of The McGraw·Hill Companies*

1 2 3 4 5 6 7 8 9 0  HPC/HPC  0 9 8 7 6 5 4 3 2 1

ISBN 0-658-00110-8 (hardcover)
ISBN 0-658-00111-6 (paperback)

This book was set in Times Roman
Printed and bound by Hamilton Printing

Cover photograph copyright © PhotoDisc

McGraw-Hill books are available at special quantity discounts to use as premiums and sales promotions, or for use in corporate training programs. For more information, please write to the Director of Special Sales, Professional Publishing, McGraw-Hill, Two Penn Plaza, New York, NY 10121-2298. Or contact your local bookstore.

This book is printed on acid-free paper.

# CONTENTS

The military. The Foreign Service. Department of Defense
Dependents Schools. U.S. Customs. Department of Justice: Border
Patrol agents. Central Intelligence Agency. Peace Corps.
AmeriCorps—The National Service Plan. Hispanic Employment
Initiative. Student Educational Employment Program. Student
internship programs with the federal government. Firsthand
accounts. For more information.

Hotel, resort, and cruise staff. Restaurant management and staff.
Travel agents. Airline and airport personnel. Tour guides. Firsthand
accounts. For more information.

How to get started. Working conditions. Possible employers.
Firsthand accounts. For more information.

Museum studies. Medical services. Social services. Media. Research
careers. The arts. Acquiring primary skills. Firsthand accounts. For
more information.

# ABOUT THE AUTHOR

Blythe Camenson is a full-time writer with more than four dozen books to her credit, most on the subject of various careers. She is also the coauthor of *Your Novel Proposal: From Creation to Contract* (Writer's Digest Books) and director of Fiction Writer's Connection, a membership organization for new writers (www.fictionwriters.com). She spent eight years in the Persian Gulf teaching English as a foreign language at various universities and language centers.

# ACKNOWLEDGMENTS

I would like to thank the following professionals for providing insights into the world of working with languages:

James Dow, Cultural Anthropology Professor
Arthur Fern, Government and Independent Consultant
Andrea Gleason, Flight Attendant
William Kelvin, Marketing/Product Manager
Joanne Leon, Assistant Director of Sales
Delores Lunceford, Missionary
Mary Fallon Miller, Travel Agent
Mary Alice Murphy, French Instructor
Todd Schuett, EFL Instructor and Translator
Beverly Stafford, Translator
Colleen Taber, Flower Importer
Maxine Taylor, Emergency Medical Technician
Richard Turnwald, Chief Purser
Jim Van Laningham, Foreign Service Officer

# CAREERS
## IN FOREIGN LANGUAGES

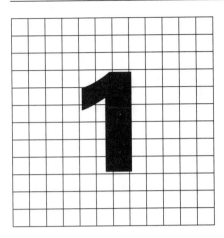

# AN INTRODUCTION TO THE FIELD

Let's assume you are bilingual or multilingual and have no problem picking up other languages. In fact, for you, learning another language is no more difficult than solving a giant jigsaw puzzle. All of the pieces are there, and you love the challenge of putting them together. Just as some people have perfect pitch, you have an ear for the sounds and patterns of another language. You can speak German, for example, or Arabic, Russian, French, Spanish—maybe even Japanese—and all without an accent. Native speakers would be surprised to learn that their language isn't your first language. You can also read and write another language fluently.

But let's not assume that English is your native language. Perhaps you were born in another country or your family is from another culture. You learned your own language and English almost simultaneously. You speak English flawlessly, even better than a native.

Your language skills are enviable, and highly marketable.

If you don't fit this profile, don't toss this book aside thinking that a career using a foreign language is outside your reach—that your language ability is just not good enough. Let's look at another scenario: You aren't a natural. You've studied a language or two in college, and your reading and speaking are passable. Your writing maybe less so. But you love the idea of other languages, other countries and cultures. Maybe you've traveled a bit, spent time in Europe, Asia, or South America. Perhaps you've even studied abroad or participated in a total immersion program for a few weeks, living with a family overseas and speaking only their language. Would that be enough to land you a job using a foreign language? Yes, for some jobs, it would.

In this book, we will look at jobs that require a foreign language as the primary skill—the reason the candidate would be hired. A translator, interpreter, or language teacher would fall into this category. These professionals must have top-notch language skills. We will also examine jobs for which foreign language fluency is a necessary but secondary skill. A sales representative for a pharmaceutical company and a software engineer for a computer company might appear to have nothing in common, but both, if bilingual, can work for enterprises with overseas interests. Their language skills will eventually come into play on business trips. Although the better their language skills, the more effective these employees will be, it's not expected that they be fully fluent. Unless, for instance, translation of important documents is required, an ability to communicate effectively and with sensitivity to the other culture will usually suffice. Their sales and design talents are valued above their language talents.

In a similar vein, those in the foreign service must pass a rigorous entrance exam that covers everything from pop culture to politics, economics to English. It does not cover a foreign language. Yet a foreign language is a real asset when working in the foreign service, and those who meet the other requirements have an edge if they have foreign language skills as well.

Another example would be the recent college graduate hired by a manufacturing firm with concerns in Asia. This student majored in languages of the Far East and is excitedly expecting a transfer to an overseas posting. Chances are, though, that transfer won't be forthcoming until the new hire learns the ropes of the company stateside and understands its foreign mission. The employer wants more from its workers than a good command of a foreign language.

So, if you are worried that your limited language ability will limit you, relax.

In addition to your language ability, you most likely have expertise in another area, such as computers, science, math, or writing. It's that expertise that will get you hired. Most jobs that ask for a foreign language view that language as a secondary requirement. In fact, most employers don't want to hire someone whose only skill is language. Your knowledge of another language is an added benefit; in most cases, it's not all that's going to land you the job.

# YOUR EDUCATIONAL PREPARATION

Ideally, the acquisition of a second or third—or even fourth—language should begin at an early age. A variety of experts, from linguists to learning psychologists and others, have researched how children acquire language. Most research supports the theory that the younger you are, the easier it is to learn a language. That said, if you weren't exposed to more than one language as a child, chances are you started learning your second language in a required high school Spanish or French class and studied that language for two to four years. That's fine—your training can progress from there.

Even if the high school student isn't thinking in terms of a career, studying a second language can improve achievement in math and English and can raise entrance exam scores too—SATs, ACTs, GREs, MCATs, and LSATs. Research conducted by the Modern Language Association has shown that math and verbal SAT scores climb with each additional year of foreign language study—which means that the longer students study a foreign language, the stronger their skills to succeed in school become. Studying a foreign language can also improve analytic and interpretive capacities.

## CHOOSING A LANGUAGE

Before looking at the options for furthering your language education, let's backtrack a little. How do you decide which language or languages to study? In high school, you might not have had much choice. Latin or French. Spanish or German. But when it comes time for college or a private language training program, the choice is yours. In most cases, this choice can be based largely on your personal interest in or affinity for a particular language. You should also keep in mind the type of work you wish to pursue.

Now more than ever the United States has contacts all over the globe. Professionals in every field use a variety of languages to ensure effective international relations.

Do you live in an area where an employee bilingual in English and Spanish would be valued, no matter the job? Then the choice is obvious. If you've thought about pursuing a profession involving some sort of export/import trade with Central or South America, again, Spanish—and perhaps Portuguese—would be the logical choice.

Arabic, the language of much of North Africa and most of the Persian Gulf, is being offered by more and more universities. Government workers, business people, medical professionals, and teachers wanting to work in the Middle East would benefit from proficiency in Arabic.

Hebrew is Israel's official language, and although English is widely spoken there, workers are expected to be fluent in Hebrew.

French is the official language not only in France but in parts of the Arab world, the African continent, and the Caribbean. French is key to a body of important scientific literature encompassing mathematics, physics, biology, and chemistry, and to the study of literature, films, and filmmaking.

Italian interests students of religion, music, opera, art, or architecture. Italy and the United States also share a fruitful trade exchange, making Italian a useful language to master.

The former Soviet Union is now wide open for trade and for the exchange of technical and scientific knowledge. To compete successfully and to keep abreast of current developments in that part of the world, the mastery of Russian is crucial.

German is the language of science, particularly engineering, not only in Germany but in Scandinavian and Eastern European countries as well. In addition to the cultural interest in Germany, trade is also extensive.

Chinese presents the biggest challenge to the American student. It's spoken by more than one billion people, but its tones and thousands of characters are difficult to master. Enrollment in Chinese language programs is on the rise, however—not only in the United States but in China, Taiwan, Singapore, and Hong Kong.

Japanese is more and more a language for finance and economics. Today it is one of the most popular languages among American students, outside the Romance languages.

Portuguese, Swahili, American Sign Language, Navajo, and 121 other languages are also taught in American high schools, colleges, and universities.

**Higher Education Enrollment Figures**

Enrollment figures show the popularity of the different languages. Table 1.1 summarizes the results of the Modern Language Association's fall 1998 survey of foreign language registration in U.S. institutions of higher education. It reflects responses from 924 two-year colleges and 1,543 four-year institutions.

**Table 1.1    Foreign Language Registrations (Undergraduate and Graduate) at Four-Year Institutions**

| Language | 1995 | 1998 |
|---|---|---|
| Spanish | 443,069 | 477,086 |
| French | 174,836 | 169,257 |
| German | 84,574 | 77,375 |
| Italian | 37,330 | 42,141 |
| Japanese | 35,294 | 33,922 |
| Latin | 25,070 | 25,305 |
| Chinese | 22,008 | 23,692 |
| Russian | 22,729 | 21,505 |
| Ancient Greek | 16,051 | 16,209 |
| Hebrew | 12,308 | 15,300 |
| Portuguese | 6,069 | 6,446 |
| American Sign Language | 910 | 4,417 |
| Arabic | 4,248 | 4,347 |
| Korean | 3,174 | 3,855 |
| Other languages | 14,400 | 15,450 |

Spanish enjoys the highest enrollments, and they are rising steadily. Enrollments in French and German have declined slightly, while American Sign Language and Hebrew show the biggest increase in recent years.

## UNIVERSITY LANGUAGE PROGRAMS

Depending on your major, university requirements for a bachelor's degree usually include at least two semesters of a language. But if you want to master a language to use it as a primary or secondary skill in a job, you'll need more than two semesters of study. The first two semesters of a college language program generally cover grammar. From the third semester onward, attention moves to reading and writing.

It's important to spread your language learning over the four years you spend in college. If you fulfill the language requirements for your degree early on, at the fourth semester, say, you risk losing your skills over the next two years. Foreign language retention weakens over time. The old adage "use it or lose it" fits well here. Make sure the university you enroll in offers enough courses to fill your schedule for four years, even if you are majoring in another subject.

## INTENSIVE LANGUAGE COURSES

Perhaps you noticed that only grammar, reading, and writing were mentioned earlier. Speaking, an important aspect of career language usage, is sorely neglected in most secondary and tertiary programs in the United States. Unless schooled in a bilingual area such as south Florida, the southwestern United States, or parts of Canada, most language students do not graduate with speaking fluency.

To remedy that, serious language students may pursue additional options, one of which is enrollment in an intensive language program, either at home or abroad. An Internet search will provide hundreds of links for language programs in the United States and overseas. One particularly good site for the latter is www.goabroad.com. There you'll find extensive directories for study abroad programs, language schools, international internships, volunteer abroad opportunities, teaching positions worldwide, and international employment. The Berlitz schools are another good resource, with more than 200 programs offered around the world. More information on these programs can be found at www.berlitz.com.

**How Intensive Language Programs Work**

Instructors in most intensive language programs usually expect their students to speak only the language being studied. The instructor uses that language as well. In addition to conversation and textbooks, some programs may offer CALL methods—computer-assisted language learning. The emphasis is on speaking, although reading, writing, and grammar are also addressed. The classroom can become a microcosm of the culture, even serving meals and showing films of the particular country.

Classes usually are held five days a week, if not more, and the day can be quite full—from four to eight hours of instruction. Often breaks for meals are conducted in the language being studied, and students are encouraged to speak it in the evenings and on weekends. Intensive language programs often provide housing as part of the package; students can room together in dormitories or with host families.

Courses run anywhere from two or three weeks to two or three months. Costs depend on the length of the program and the type of housing you opt for. Fire up your favorite search engines and you'll be able to find out about all the available options and the costs involved.

## STUDYING ABROAD

Although much of your initial language study most likely will be conducted on home turf, many students opt for a stint overseas, whether through a junior year abroad program or at a language school during the summer months. Studying overseas almost guarantees an immersion situation. Most students report a marked improvement in at least their speaking skills after studying abroad.

Costs vary with each school or program. In addition to tuition and the cost of textbooks, expenses will include round-trip airfare, room and board, local transportation, and various other personal expenses such as movie or theater tickets, or souvenirs from shopping expeditions. Some programs also expect you to pay for short-term health insurance, although this might be waived if your own policy covers you while you are abroad.

Study abroad programs are costly and may be beyond the budget of many students and recent graduates. But they are well worth pursuing. For the serious, career-minded individual with a strong desire to master a language, a course overseas is a necessity, not a luxury.

## SUPPLEMENTAL STUDY

Language programs—even intensive and full immersion arrangements—are not enough to fully master the nuances and idioms of a foreign language. Supplement your course work and conversation with native speakers, with anything that will increase your proficiency. While overseas or by perusing newsstands in this country or Internet sources, locate and read a variety of foreign language magazines, newspapers, and books. In addition, listen to foreign music and watch foreign films (without the subtitles).

Learning a language takes time, patience, and persistence. The more you practice, the more proficient you'll become.

## FOR MORE INFORMATION

Please refer to the appendixes and to the resources at the end of each chapter for additional educational and career information.

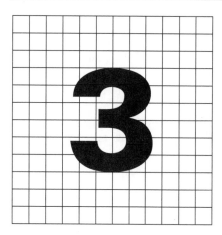

# TEACHING LANGUAGES

Teaching languages is perhaps the first career path a foreign language aficionado would think to travel down. Most of us have been exposed to language teaching in school, and it could very well be this early exposure that inspires someone to pursue the field.

While you may only vaguely understand the other careers open to people with a language background—at least until you finish this book—teaching is something known, something familiar. To many, it's a very attractive life. Teachers acquire a body of knowledge and exchange ideas with students and with other teachers. Good teachers often remark that they learn as much from their students as their students learn from them. Language teachers also have an added bonus of continued opportunities for travel and cultural exchange. Depending upon the setting, teachers often work a nine- or ten-month contract and use their ample summer vacations for more travel or study.

Good language teachers impart an excitement to their students. Some foreign language students will just be fulfilling a high school or college language requirement, but many others will be pursuing the language more seriously— and enjoying it. A taste of French or German or Spanish and the culture that goes along with it might be all a student needs to pack up his or her backpack and log on to a discount ticket Internet site. Good language teachers focus not only on the language but on the culture and the tolerance the study of it instills. Those who choose to speak another language and learn about other peoples are usually sensitive to and appreciative of differences in lifestyle. In fact, it's the cultural differences rather than the similarities that make teaching language so attractive.

With the growing focus in this country on international business and trade, foreign language acquisition is increasingly important. Although many students in North America will never need to use a language outside the classroom, more and more people will be entering careers that require a second language, if not as a primary skill, then certainly as a secondary one.

As a result of the attention given to foreign language _____ in the past decade or so, the curriculum at the elementary school lev____ ___ en modified to include language instruction. Young people learn a langu____ __ h more easily than adults. When the subject matter is presented in a f____ d challenging way, children become sponges, quickly absorbing what they a.e taught. When these students enter middle school and high school, they have already had several years of language instruction. This has resulted in modifications and expansions of secondary school curricula to accommodate these advanced students. And the more foreign language students there are, the better the career outlook for you, the teacher.

## CAREER OUTLOOK FOR LANGUAGE TEACHERS

**Elementary and Secondary**

The job market for teachers varies widely by geographic area, subject specialty, and type of school. Many inner cities (often characterized by overcrowded conditions and higher than average crime and poverty rates) and rural areas (characterized by their remote location and relatively low salaries) have difficulty attracting enough teachers, so job prospects should continue to be better in these areas than in suburban districts.

Currently, many school districts have difficulty hiring qualified teachers in some subjects, including bilingual education. With enrollments of minorities increasing and minority teachers in short supply, efforts to recruit minority teachers should intensify. Also, the number of non-English-speaking students has grown dramatically, especially in California and Florida, which have large Spanish-speaking student populations, creating demand for bilingual teachers and those who teach English as a second language. (You will learn more about teaching English to speakers of other languages later in this chapter.) Teachers who are geographically mobile and who are licensed in more than one subject should have a distinct advantage in finding a job.

Overall employment of elementary and secondary school teachers is expected to increase about as fast as the average for all occupations through 2008. The retirement of a large number of teachers currently in their forties and fifties should open up many additional jobs. The demand for teachers is also dependent on state and local expenditures for education. Pressures from taxpayers to limit spending could result in less demand than projected; pressures to spend more to improve the quality of education could increase the teacher workforce.

In anticipation of growing student enrollments at the secondary school level, many states are implementing policies that will encourage more students to become teachers. Some are giving large signing bonuses that are distributed over the teacher's first few years of teaching. Some are expanding state scholarships, issuing loans for moving expenses, and implementing loan-forgiveness programs, allowing education majors with at least a B average to receive state-paid tuition as long as they agree to teach in the state for four years.

The supply of teachers also is expected to increase in response to reports of improved job prospects, more teacher involvement in school policy, and greater public interest in education. In recent years, the total number of bachelor's and master's degrees granted in education has steadily increased. In addition, more teachers will be drawn from a reserve pool of career changers; substitute teachers; and teachers completing alternative certification programs, relocating to different schools, and reentering the workforce.

**College and University**

Employment of college and university faculty is expected to increase faster than the average for all occupations through 2008 as enrollments in higher education increase. Many additional openings will arise as faculty members retire. Nevertheless, prospective job applicants should expect to face competition, particularly for full-time, tenure-track positions at four-year institutions.

Since 1998, the traditional college-age (18 to 24) population has been growing again after several years of decline. This population increase, along with a higher proportion of eighteen- to twenty-four-year-olds attending college and a growing number of part-time, female, minority, and older students, will spur college enrollments. Enrollment is projected to rise from 14.6 million in 1998 to 16.1 million in 2008, an increase of about 10 percent. Growing numbers of students will necessitate hiring more faculty. At the same time, many faculty will be retiring, opening up even more positions. Also, the number of doctorate degrees is expected to grow more slowly than in the past, somewhat easing the competition for some faculty positions. Still, many in the academic community are concerned that institutions will increasingly favor the hiring of adjunct faculty over full-time, tenure-track faculty. For many years, keen competition for faculty jobs has forced some applicants to accept part-time academic appointments that offer little hope of tenure and others to seek nonacademic positions. Many colleges, faced with reduced state funding and growing numbers of part-time and older students, increased the hiring of adjunct and part-time faculty to save money on pay and benefits and to accommodate the needs of nontraditional students.

According to a survey conducted by the Modern Language Association, in English and foreign language departments and especially in Ph.D.-granting departments, first-year courses are often taught almost entirely by part- or full-time non-tenure-track faculty members and (where they are available) graduate student instructors. If funding remains tight over the projection period, this trend is likely to continue. Because of uncertainty about future funding sources, some colleges and universities are also controlling costs by changing the mix of academic programs offered, eliminating some programs altogether, and increasing class size.

Overall, job prospects will continue to be better in certain fields—business, engineering, health science, and computer science, for example—that offer attractive nonacademic job opportunities and attract fewer applicants for academic positions. Also, excellent job prospects in a field—for example, computer science—result in higher student enrollments, increasing faculty needs in that field. On the other hand, poor job prospects in a field, such as history in recent years, discourage students and reduce demand for faculty.

In summary, because graduation requirements in language are being reintroduced in many institutions across the country, the number of students in language courses is likely to increase, thus increasing the need for language teachers. However, these teachers will most likely be part-time adjunct or full-time non-tenure-track instructors.

## WORKING CONDITIONS FOR LANGUAGE TEACHERS

Although language teachers share a similar body of knowledge and may use similar methods in the classroom, the conditions under which they work will vary by the institution, the type of school, the age of the students, and the motivation of the students.

**Public Schools**

Seeing students develop new skills and gain an appreciation of knowledge and learning can be very rewarding. However, teaching may be frustrating when it entails dealing with unmotivated and disrespectful students. Occasionally, teachers must cope with unruly behavior and violence in the schools. Teachers may also experience stress when dealing with large classes, students from disadvantaged or multicultural backgrounds, and heavy workloads. They are sometimes isolated from their colleagues because they work alone in a classroom of students. However, some schools are allowing teachers to work in teams and with mentors to enhance their professional development.

Including school duties performed outside the classroom, many teachers work more than forty hours a week. Most teachers work the traditional ten-month school year, with a two-month summer vacation. Those on the ten-month schedule may teach in summer sessions, take other jobs, travel, or pursue other personal interests. Many enroll in college courses or workshops to continue their education. Teachers in districts with a year-round schedule typically work eight-week sessions separated by one week of vacation, with five weeks for midwinter break.

Most states have tenure laws that prevent teachers from being fired without just cause and due process. Teachers may obtain tenure after they have satisfactorily completed a probationary period, normally three years. Tenure does not absolutely guarantee a job, but it does provide some security.

**Colleges and Universities**

College faculty usually have flexible schedules. They must be present for classes, usually twelve to sixteen hours per week, and for faculty and committee meetings. Most establish regular office hours for student consultations, usually three to six hours per week. Otherwise, faculty are free to decide when and where they will work, and how much time to devote to course preparation, grading, study, research, graduate student supervision, and other activities.

Adjusting to these responsibilities can be challenging as new faculty switch roles from student to teacher. Some institutions offer career development programs to ease the transition. This adjustment may be even more difficult should class sizes grow in response to faculty and budget cutbacks, increasing an instructor's workload. Also, with many institutions increasing their reliance on part-time faculty, who usually have limited administrative and student advising duties, the declining number of full-time faculty are left with a heavier workload.

Some faculty members work staggered hours and teach night and weekend classes. This is particularly true for those who teach at two-year community colleges or institutions with large enrollments of older students with full-time jobs or family responsibilities. Most colleges and universities require faculty to work nine months of the year—which allows them the time to teach additional courses, do research, travel, or pursue nonacademic interests during the summer and school holidays. Colleges and universities usually have funds to support faculty research or other professional development needs, including travel to conferences and research sites.

Faculty may experience a conflict between their responsibilities to teach students and the pressure to do research and publish their findings. This may be a particular problem for young faculty seeking advancement in four-year research universities. However, growing emphasis on undergraduate teaching performance in tenure decisions may alleviate some of this pressure.

Part-time faculty usually spend little time on campus because they do not have an office. In addition, they may teach at more than one college, traveling between them, earning the name "gypsy faculty." Part-time faculty are usually ineligible for tenure. For those seeking full-time employment in academia, this lack of job security can be stressful.

## Private Language Centers

Conditions vary, but in general, full-time teachers at private language centers conduct more classes and work more hours than their counterparts working in the school systems or in colleges and universities. Salaries can be offered on an hourly basis, with no added benefits.

## Foreign Language Tutoring

Language specialists can also find part-time work tutoring foreign students who have language difficulties. Tutors can offer individual or group lessons. You can advertise your services in student newspapers; on bulletin boards, especially in the international student office; and through word of mouth. Some university modern language departments keep a list of paid tutors to which you can add your name.

## OVERSEAS EMPLOYMENT INFORMATION FOR LANGUAGE TEACHERS

Working conditions overseas vary drastically from those in the United States. (Teaching English as a foreign language abroad is covered later in this chapter.) The following list has been prepared by the U.S. government in response to the numerous inquiries received from American teachers. It consists primarily of points of contact for teaching positions in overseas elementary and secondary schools and is limited to organizations that recruit or employ a large number of teachers. Additional information on teaching abroad for U.S. government concerns is provided in Chapter 5.

**International Educational Exchange Program (Fulbright-Hays Act)— Teaching in Elementary and Secondary Schools**
Teacher Exchange Section
U.S. Office of Education
U.S. Department of Health, Education, and Welfare
Washington, DC 20418

**University Lecturing and Advanced Research**
Conference Board of Associated Research Councils
Committee on International Exchange of Persons
2101 Constitution Avenue NW
Washington, DC 20418

**Teaching Assistantships and Fellowships for Study and Research**
Institute of International Education
709 New York Avenue NW
Washington, DC 20006

Institute of International Education
809 United Nations Plaza
New York, NY 10017

**United States Information Agency—Teachers of English as a Foreign Language, Directors of Courses, and Administrators in Binational Centers**
Recruitment and Source Development Staff
Office of Personnel and Training
United States Information Agency
1776 Pennsylvania Avenue NW
Washington, DC 20547

**Peace Corps—Teaching in elementary, secondary, normal, and vocational schools and in universities**
(No teaching experience required.)

Director of Recruitment, Peace Corps
806 Connecticut Avenue NW
Washington, DC 20525

**International Schools Services—Teaching in American-sponsored, community-sponsored, privately operated, or company-sponsored schools**
(Some positions for guidance counselors, librarians, curriculum specialists, and administrators.)

International Schools Services
126 Alexander Street
Princeton, NJ 08540

American Samoa
Director of Education
Department of Education
Pago Pago, American Samoa 96920

Canal Zone Division of Schools
Balboa Heights, Canal Zone
Guam Assistant Superintendent—
    Personnel
Department of Education
Government of Guam
Agana, Guam 96910

Guam DOD Domestic Elementary and
    Secondary Schools (DDESS)
Bldg. FH01 ComNavMar
Haputo Road
Santa Rita, Guam 96915

Pacific Islands Personnel Officer
Office of High Commissioner
Trust Territory of the Pacific Islands
Saipan, Mariana Islands

Puerto Rico Secretary of Education
Department of Education
Hato Rey, Puerto Rico 00900

Commissioner of Education
Department of Education
Charlotte Amalie (St. Thomas)
Virgin Islands 00801

State of Hawaii Superintendent Department of Education
P.O. Box 2360
Honolulu, Hawaii 96804

## TRAINING FOR LANGUAGE TEACHERS

**Secondary School Teachers**

All fifty states and the District of Columbia require public school teachers to be licensed. (Licensure is not required for teachers in private schools.) Usually licensure is granted by the state board of education or a licensure advisory committee. Teachers may be licensed to teach the early childhood grades (usually nursery school through grade 3), the elementary grades (grades 1 through 6 or 8), the middle grades (grades 5 through 8), a secondary education subject area such as a foreign language (usually grades 7 through 12), or a special subject, such as reading or music (usually grades K through 12).

Requirements for regular licenses vary by state, although many have reciprocity agreements that make it easier for teachers licensed in one state to become licensed in another. All states require a bachelor's degree and completion of an approved teacher training program with a prescribed number of subject and education credits, as well as supervised practice teaching. About one-third also require technology training as part of the teacher certification process. A number of states require specific minimum grade point averages for teacher licensure. Some require teachers to obtain a master's degree in education, which involves at least one year of additional course work beyond the bachelor's degree with specialization in a particular subject.

Almost all states require that applicants for teacher licensure be tested for competency in basic skills such as reading, writing, teaching, and subject matter proficiency. Most states also require continuing education for renewal of the teacher's license. Increasingly, states are moving toward performance-based standards for licensure. Teachers must pass a rigorous comprehensive teaching examination to obtain a provisional license, then demonstrate satisfactory performance over an extended period of time to obtain a full license.

Many states offer alternative teacher licensure programs for people who have bachelor's degrees in the subject they will teach but lack the education courses required for a regular license. These programs were originally designed to ease teacher shortages in certain subjects, such as mathematics and science. The programs have expanded to attract more people into teaching, including recent college graduates and career changers. In some programs, individuals begin teaching quickly under provisional licensure. After working under the close supervision of experienced educators for one or two years while taking education courses outside school hours, they receive full licensure if they have progressed satisfactorily. Under other programs, college graduates who do not meet licensure requirements need to take only those courses they lack. This may take one or two semesters of full-time study. States may issue emergency licenses to individuals who do not meet the requirements when schools cannot attract enough qualified teachers to fill positions. Programs that grant a master's degree in education as well as a license are available.

For several years, the National Board for Professional Teaching Standards has offered voluntary national certification for teachers. To become nationally certified, teachers must prove their aptitude by compiling a portfolio showing their work in the classroom and by passing a written evaluation of their teaching knowledge. They may become certified in one of seven areas. These areas are based on the age of the students and, in some cases, subject area. For example, teachers may become certified to teach a foreign language to early adolescents (ages 11 to 15) or as early childhood generalists. All states recognize national certification, and many states and school districts give teachers holding national certification special benefits. Benefits typically include higher salaries and reimbursement for continuing education and certification fees. Additionally, many states allow nationally certified teachers to carry a license from one state to another.

The National Council for Accreditation of Teacher Education currently accredits more than five hundred teacher education programs across the United States. Four-year colleges typically require students to wait until their sophomore year before applying for admission to teacher education programs. Aspiring secondary school teachers either major in the foreign language they plan to teach while also taking education courses, or major in education and take courses in the foreign language. Most programs require students to perform a student teaching internship. To maintain accreditation, teacher education programs are now required to include classes in the use of computers and other technologies.

Many states now offer professional development schools, which are partnerships between universities and elementary or secondary schools. Students enter these one-year programs after completing their bachelor's degree. Professional development schools merge theory with practice and allow the student to experience a year of teaching firsthand, with professional guidance.

Teachers may become administrators or supervisors, although the number of these positions is limited and competition can be intense. In some school systems, highly qualified, experienced teachers can become senior or mentor teachers with higher pay and additional responsibilities. They guide and assist less-experienced teachers while keeping most of their own teaching responsibilities.

**College and University**     Most college and university faculty fall into one of four academic ranks: professor, associate professor, assistant professor, and instructor. These positions are usually considered to be tenure-track positions. A small number of faculty, called lecturers, usually are not on the tenure track. Most faculty members are hired as instructors or assistant professors.

Four-year colleges and universities usually consider doctoral degree holders for full-time, tenure-track positions but may hire master's degree holders or doctoral candidates for certain disciplines, such as foreign languages and the arts, or for part-time and temporary jobs. At two-year colleges, master's degree holders fill most full-time positions. However, with increasing competition for available jobs, institutions can be more selective in their hiring practices. Master's degree holders may find it difficult to obtain employment as they are passed over in favor of candidates holding a Ph.D. Some Ph.D.s extend or take new postdoctoral appointments if they are unable to find a faculty job. Most of these appointments offer a nominal salary.

Doctoral programs take an average of four to eight years of full-time study beyond the bachelor's degree (including time spent completing a master's degree and a dissertation). Some programs, such as those in the humanities, take longer to complete; others, such as those in engineering, usually are shorter. Doctoral programs include twenty or more increasingly specialized courses and seminars plus comprehensive examinations on all major areas of the field. Candidates also must complete a dissertation—a written report of original research in the candidate's major field of study. It sets forth an original hypothesis or proposes a model and tests it. Students in the natural sciences and engineering usually do laboratory work; in the humanities, they study original documents and other published material. The dissertation, done under the guidance of one or more faculty advisors, usually takes one or two years of full-time work.

A major step in the traditional academic career is attaining tenure. New tenure-track faculty are usually hired as instructors or assistant professors and must serve a certain period (usually seven years) under term contracts. At the end of the contract period, their record of teaching, research, and overall contribution to the institution is reviewed; tenure is granted if the review is favorable. According to the American Association of University Professors, in 1998–99 about 65 percent of all full-time faculty held tenure, and about 86 percent were in tenure-track positions. Those denied tenure usually must leave the institution.

Tenured professors cannot be fired without just cause and due process. Tenure protects the faculty's academic freedom—their ability to teach and conduct research without fear of being fired for advocating unpopular ideas. It also gives both faculty and institutions the stability needed for effective research and teaching and provides financial security for faculty. Some institutions have adopted post-tenure review policies to encourage ongoing evaluation of faculty.

The number of tenure-track positions is expected to decline as institutions seek flexibility in dealing with financial matters and changing student interests. Institutions will rely more heavily on limited term contracts and part-time faculty, shrinking the total pool of tenured faculty. Some institutions offer limited term contracts to prospective faculty, typically two-, three-, or five-year full-time contracts. These contracts may be terminated or extended at the end of the period. Institutions are not obligated to grant tenure to these contract holders.

In addition, some institutions have limited the percentage of faculty who can be tenured.

Some faculty—based on teaching experience, research, publication, and service on campus committees and task forces—move into administrative and managerial positions, such as departmental chairperson, dean, and president. At four-year institutions, such advancement requires a doctoral degree. At two-year colleges, a doctorate is helpful but not usually required, except for advancement to some top administrative positions.

## PH.D. FOREIGN LANGUAGE EMPLOYMENT FIGURES

Every ten years, the Modern Language Association conducts a series of surveys of Ph.D.-granting departments in the United States concerning job placement of their doctoral graduates in English, foreign languages, comparative literature, linguistics, and classics. The most recent survey covers those who were awarded degrees between September 1, 1996, and August 31, 1997.

The following table shows the job placement for foreign language Ph.D.s (1996–1997).

**Table 3.1   Job Placement**

| | |
|---|---|
| ***Teaching in Higher Education*** | |
| Full-time non-tenure-track, renewable appointment | 18.4% |
| Full-time non-tenure-track, 1-year appointment | 8.3% |
| Part-time employment | 8.8% |
| | |
| ***Other Higher Education Placement*** | |
| Postdoctoral fellowship | 1.8% |
| Academic administration | 1.1% |
| | |
| ***Employed Outside Higher Education*** | |
| Secondary or elementary | 3.4% |
| School teaching in government, for-profit, or not-for-profit organization | 5.0% |
| Self-employed | .6% |
| Not employed or seeking employment | 8.3% |
| Not seeking employment | 1.3% |
| Teaching, classification unknown | 2.6% |

## FINDING A JOB

Finding jobs within the public school system has always entailed contacting individual principals or contacting school boards for countywide listings. Some school boards will take applications only when there is an opening; others will keep applications on file. In most cases an application would be followed by a personal interview.

One of the best known methods for job hunting at the college level is through the *Chronicle of Higher Education*, a weekly periodical that accepts ads for openings in every field across the country. Jobs are also listed at their website: www.chronicle.com.

For a job listing specific to foreign languages, try the Modern Language Association (MLA) site at www.mla.org. If you're willing to relocate and not set on a particular area of the country, finding a job in a college or university will be easier.

The MLA Job Information Service has helped candidates for faculty appointments locate positions and kept the profession informed about hiring trends since 1971. Operated by the MLA in cooperation with the Association of Departments of English (ADE) and the Association of Departments of Foreign Languages (ADFL), the service provides a central source of notices about faculty openings in postsecondary English and foreign language departments. The searchable electronic database is made available by subscription over the World Wide Web. Subscribers may be individuals, English and foreign language departments (as part of membership in ADE and ADFL), or libraries. Subscription terms and on-line access differ for each category of subscriber and are described at the site.

A search on the Web will uncover other sites with job listings, most of them free.

## SALARIES FOR TEACHERS

**Secondary**

Median annual earnings of kindergarten, elementary, and secondary school teachers ranged from $33,590 to $37,890 in 1998. The lowest 10 percent ranged from $19,710 to $24,390, and the top 10 percent, $53,720 to $70,030. According to the American Federation of Teachers, beginning teachers with a bachelor's degree earn an average of $25,700. The estimated average salary of all public elementary and secondary school teachers in the 1997–98 school year was $39,300.

Private school teachers generally earn less than public school teachers. In some schools, teachers receive extra pay for coaching sports and working with students in extracurricular activities. Some teachers earn extra income during the summer working in the school system or in other jobs.

**College and University**

Median annual earnings of college and university faculty in 1998 were $46,630. The middle 50 percent earned between $33,390 and $71,360. The lowest 10 percent earned less than $23,100, and the highest 10 percent, more than $90,360.

Earnings vary according to faculty rank and type of institution, geographic area, and field. According to a 1998–99 survey by the American Association of University Professors, salaries for full-time faculty averaged $56,300. By rank, the average for professors was $72,700; associate professors, $53,200; assistant professors, $43,800; instructors, $33,400; and lecturers, $37,200. Faculty in four-year institutions earn higher salaries, on average, than those in two-year schools. Average salaries for faculty in public institutions ($55,900) were lower in 1998–99 than those for private independent institutions ($63,500) but higher than those for religiously affiliated private colleges and universities ($49,400). In fields with high-paying nonacademic alternatives—notably medicine and law but also engineering and business, among others—earnings exceed these averages. In others—such as the humanities and education—they are lower. Most faculty members have significant earnings in addition to their base salary, from consulting, teaching additional courses, researching, writing for publication, or other employment.

Most full-time college and university faculty enjoy unique benefits, including access to campus facilities, tuition waivers for dependents, housing and travel allowances, and paid sabbatical leaves. Part-time faculty usually go without most of these benefits, including health insurance, retirement benefits, and sabbatical leave.

## TEACHING ENGLISH TO SPEAKERS OF OTHER LANGUAGES

TESOL—Teaching English to Speakers of Other Languages—is a professional organization for teachers of English as a second language. In TESOL English is the language of instruction, and knowledge of a foreign language is in no way necessary to enter the profession. But understanding how language is acquired and sensitivity to foreign cultures are essential to a successful career. Those residing and working overseas as they teach English will find knowledge of the local language helpful in day-to-day living.

**The Difference Between ESL and EFL**

ESL stands for English as a second language; TESL for teaching English as a second language. ESL students may be immigrants or refugees to an English-speaking country who need to learn the language to cope with daily life.

EFL stands for English as a foreign language; TEFL for teaching English as a foreign language. EFL students may live in a country where their own language is the primary tongue but where English is used for academic study, when traveling to an English-speaking country, or for business purposes.

Some professionals feel there are critical differences between ESL and EFL in teaching methods and approach. A few recognized differences between the disciplines are:

- EFL learners generally spend fewer hours per week studying English than their ESL counterparts in settings within English-speaking countries.

- EFL learners have little exposure to English outside the classroom and also have little need or opportunity to practice their newly acquired language skills.

- A classroom of EFL learners has a common native-language background. ESL classes generally comprise students from a variety of countries.

**What an ESL/EFL Teacher Does**

Many people unfamiliar with the profession believe that since they speak English, they can teach it. As mentioned earlier, in some locations that's true, and travelers wanting to earn extra money to help pay for their trip often find work tutoring or providing practice in conversation skills. But as the number of professionally trained teachers increases, opportunities for unqualified teachers decreases.

Professional ESL/EFL teachers go through a variety of training programs, studying methodology, second language acquisition, curriculum design, research methods, and basic language skills. They might also add particular specializations to their program, such as computer-assisted language learning (CALL) or the use of video in the classroom.

ESL/EFL teachers instruct students in basic English language skills: reading, writing, listening, and conversation. Like all teachers, they are responsible for designing lesson plans and for administering and grading tests. They might also help develop the teaching program that will best meet their particular students' needs, writing materials to be used in the classroom.

**Employment Outlook**

It's estimated that more than one thousand million people around the world speak or are studying English. They choose to learn English for a number of reasons: to attend colleges and universities in English-speaking countries, to ensure better business communications, to enhance employability, to facilitate government relations, to create a more rewarding travel experience, or for many, to be able to communicate day-to-day in the English-speaking country in which they live.

In the United States alone, close to three million nonnative English speakers with limited English proficiency are enrolled in U.S. public schools grades K through 12. Enrollment in adult ESL programs is approximately 1.5 million. These are low estimates. Also, although it would be impossible to document all the potential language learners not enrolled in any ESL program, some programs report long waiting lists. In short, the number of people in the United States desiring ESL instruction is on the rise. As the public school systems, government agencies, and private enterprises work toward filling the demand, opportunities for ESL/EFL teachers will continue to grow.

**ESL/EFL Qualifications and Requirements**

The field of teaching English as a second or foreign language (TESL/TEFL) has grown enormously in the past two decades. At one time, it was believed that the only qualification necessary to teach English to nonnative speakers was to be a native speaker yourself. Today, that school of thought has almost vanished. Before TESOL firmly established itself as an important and valid discipline, an individual who ventured overseas could find tutoring and part-time teaching work along the way to cover travel and living expenses. Although such situations still exist in a few locations, they are quickly shrinking, replaced by quality programs touting qualified and experienced ESL/EFL teachers.

When deciding how much training to pursue, take into account the level of teaching you plan to do. Classroom teachers working within U.S. school systems, for example, need at least a B.A.; overseas university language center instructors are usually expected to have earned an M.A.

**Bachelor's degree.** A bachelor's degree is the basic requirement for employment. If the candidate expects to go on for a master's degree, the B.A. need not be in TESOL. An undergraduate could major in English or foreign languages or international relations. But if the B.A. is to be the terminal degree, the program should cover courses such as the grammatical, phonological, and semantic systems of the English language, methodology and second language assessment, the study of another language and its cultural system, and practice teaching.

**Teacher certification.** Most states require certification for teaching ESL at the elementary and secondary levels in public schools. Contact your state board of education to learn what the certification requirements are. University teacher training programs will offer the required courses. A listing of state certification/endorsement licensing requirements is provided in TESOL's Directory of Professional Preparation Programs in the United States. TESOL's address is provided at the end of this chapter.

**U.S. certificate.** After earning a bachelor's degree, another eighteen to twenty-one graduate credits can end in an ESL certificate, which is offered by many universities with teacher training programs. The U.S. certificate is adequate for many job settings outside the United States and would qualify you to teach adult education, in private language programs, or at some community colleges within the United States.

**U.K. certification.** These days, many American as well as British teachers are earning TEFL certificates in the United Kingdom. The RSA/Cambridge certificate can open doors in the world of TESOL. It can be earned in short-term intensive programs throughout the United Kingdom. For a complete listing of these programs, refer to the EFL Career Guide, published by EFL Limited, 64 Ormly Road, Ramsey, Isle of Man, U.K. Write directly to the program of your choice for applications, deadlines, requirements, and costs.

**Master's degree.** A master's degree, in addition to providing a theoretical background, will prepare you in classroom teaching methods, curriculum development, materials writing, and to some extent, program coordination. A master's degree will qualify you to teach in most settings in the United States and abroad.

There are a variety of names for the different master's degrees including M.A. in TESOL, M.Ed. in TESOL, M.A. or M.S. in applied linguistics, M.A.T. in TESOL, or an M.A. in English with an emphasis in TESOL. An employer might specify a particular degree when advertising a position but is usually willing to consider any of the variations.

**Doctorate.** Those wishing to advance academically and become involved in language research, writing for professional publications, and/or teaching future ESL/EFL teachers at the master's level will need to pursue a Ph.D.

TESOL's Directory of Professional Preparation Programs in the United States lists U.S. universities offering certificate, master's, and Ph.D. programs in TESOL.

Before making a serious commitment in terms of the number of years of training you will pursue, you can follow a few other options first to get a feel for the profession:

- Volunteer your time and take advantage of any in-house training the organization might offer.

- Enroll in a short-term intensive training program and work toward a certificate.

- After finishing your bachelor's degree, spend a year or two working in the field before going on for a master's.

Whatever you choose to do, it's best to start with a plan. If you ask a handful of longtime ESL/EFL teachers how they got started, you might hear a string of similar and somewhat surprising answers. Here are some examples:

"I fell into it; it wasn't something I had originally planned."

"I started off volunteering while I was pursuing another profession. I ended up staying in ESL."

"I did some tutoring when I was traveling in Europe and one thing led to another. I went back later to get my master's degree."

"I took a summer job at a U.S. language institute; it helped me to get a teaching job overseas, and that job led to another job."

"I don't have any TEFL qualifications. My master's degree is in English literature, but I was hired anyway. Now, after ten years of overseas experience, I can work almost anywhere."

"My bachelor's is in French. While I was studying in Paris eight years ago, I met an EFL teacher at a language school there. There was an unexpected opening and I just fell into it."

"It wasn't something I planned; I just fell into it."

"I just fell into it . . ."

Many teachers who started out ten or more years ago will probably have similar responses. Teaching ESL/EFL was something they just fell into. But times have changed. These days, to land the plum jobs, teachers plan their programs very carefully. They choose courses that will meet their own needs and interests, while also considering the needs and requirements of future employers.

**ESL/EFL Job Settings**

As the need for English language instruction increases, so does the variety of locations in which ESL/EFL teachers can work. TESOLers are finding their skills more and more in demand, and the better their qualifications, the better their employment outlook.

ESL teachers usually work in the United States with students from varied cultures and language backgrounds. They teach students who have come here to study, work, or live. They teach day and evening classes through adult education programs, work as certified teachers in the public school systems at the elementary and secondary levels, or instruct incoming international students at university-based language centers. They also find work in private language schools teaching students from around the world.

Areas of the country that have been most impacted by refugees or immigration offer the most opportunities for employment. Major cities, such as San Diego, Los Angeles, San Francisco, and Seattle on the west coast and Miami, Washington, D.C., Baltimore, New York, and Boston on the east coast, have more private and government-funded language instruction programs than other U.S. locations. That said, most U.S. universities have an international student population, from Asia or the Middle East, for example, and require teachers to staff their language centers.

EFL teachers work overseas in international schools, for overseas companies or private U.S. companies with overseas concerns, for the Peace Corps, or for U.S. government centers for English language instruction based around the world.

ESL/EFL teachers can find employment almost anywhere. Jobs appear to be concentrated in the United States; in Middle Eastern countries such as Saudi Arabia; in the Far East in countries such as Japan, Hong Kong, China, and South Korea; in Central and Eastern Europe in Turkey and Poland; in North Africa in Egypt and Morocco; and in the many countries of Central and South America.

Teaching environments and work conditions vary widely. An ESL/EFL teacher could find herself working in a modern classroom outfitted with state-of-the-art equipment and teaching aids—overhead and slide projectors, computers, VCRs and videos—or in a primitive setting with tin-roofed buildings and outdated materials, if any at all. There could be chalkboards but no chalk, computers but only intermittent electricity. There are numerous possibilities, and all should be taken into account when deciding the conditions under which you would be most comfortable working.

## What Makes a Good ESL/EFL Teacher?

ESL/EFL teachers need to possess the same qualities all teachers do: intelligence, patience, and creativity. But teaching English as a second or foreign language is not the same as teaching it as a first language. The foundation of knowledge and methodology for this field includes linguistics, second language acquisition, education practices, sociology, anthropology, psychology, testing and measurement, and other related subjects. They must understand the nature of language and how people learn languages. They must have cross-cultural knowledge and experience as well as sensitivity to individual differences among students. In certain settings, they must also have knowledge of other areas related to international student affairs, such as immigration and visa policies.

In addition, ESL/EFL teachers must have a special talent; they carry a weight of responsibility. How they present their subject will affect their students' attitudes toward language learning, the English language in particular, and toward the country and its culture.

These further qualities are vital to a successful career as a teacher of English as a second or foreign language:

- Experience traveling or living in international settings

- Enthusiasm for the subject matter

- Independence

- A sincere appreciation of people of different cultures

- Ability to work as part of a team

- Tolerance

- Flexibility

- Maturity

- Communication skills

A successful ESL/EFL teacher also pursues continuing professional development and encourages the same in those he or she supervises, including other teachers and staff members.

But must a successful ESL/EFL teacher be a native speaker of English? Although a small contingent might argue for that requirement, most feel it is an elitist attitude that has no place in the field of TESOL. Why should every non-English-speaking country in the world have to depend on English-speaking ones for its English-language instruction? A teacher from France, for example, with a solid command of the English language and professional qualifications from a recognized TESOL program, is ultimately better equipped to help students in her own country understand the process of learning English. She will be more aware of the nuances, the specific French-to-English problems her students may have, than a native English speaker. What if she's tempted to speak French in the classroom to help a student over a rough spot? Everyone agrees that English should be the language of instruction in an ESL/EFL classroom, but most don't see the harm—in fact, can see the benefit—of an occasional quick translation to clear up points of confusion. Why waste precious classroom time when a quick aside allows everyone to move on?

**At Home or Abroad?**

Among all the other decisions future ESL/EFL teachers have to make, from training programs to individual specializations, one of the most important is that of job setting. Will you stay in the Unites States or venture abroad?

Although teaching overseas is not a requirement for a successful career, per se, the experience does greatly enhance one's employability and chances for advancement. Needless to say, the opportunity to travel or live overseas and get to know different countries in depth is one of the main reasons so many people are attracted to the profession. Teachers who opt to stay in the United States still enjoy a sort of vicarious travel by working with students from different countries.

For most teachers, the ultimate reward comes from the students themselves. This is what three ESL/EFL teachers have to say on the subject:

> "I helped prepare a Yemeni student for postgraduate study in Britain. I gave him extra tutoring in EFL and linguistics. Not only did he pass the program, he was the number-one student. It was very gratifying."

> "Rewarding moments for me were when the first group of students I had taught graduated and years later, when several students came back to see me to tell me how much I had helped them."

> "I still get letters from former students. I know that in part they want to practice their writing skills, but it feels wonderful to hear from them and see how they've improved."

Most satisfied TESOLers will tell you that the advantages far outweigh the disadvantages. Still, the few minuses to teaching work in general and ESL/EFL in particular should be considered. Foremost among them is stress. As with any profession, stress can be generated by strained relations with coworkers, work assignments outside your usual scope of duties, and occasional boredom with the subject matter. But certain stresses are endemic to the teaching profession. These include handling discipline problems in the classroom, meeting a new class for the first time, overcrowded classrooms, deadlines for grading papers or handing in exam scores, and inadequate materials or facilities. Stress can also be brought about by change, and for ESL/EFL teachers who travel abroad, adjusting to a new culture and new ways of doing things can create new levels of anxiety and tension. These levels usually decrease once the settling-in period is over, although they may escalate again upon departure.

Program administrators often suffer from stress even more than classroom teachers. Claire Monro writes in her article "Too Busy to Care Anymore: Burnout and the ESL Program Administrator" that "job-related factors can cause burnout in vulnerable ESL administrators. Foremost among these is the nature of the ESL student population. These students require more attention than native English speakers. Unfamiliar with cultural and linguistic matters both on campus and in the larger community, they often depend on empathetic ESL faculty for help. If the administrator is available more than others in the program, that person may be the one to whom students come most frequently. . . . Another possible stressor is the onus of being the unofficial spokesperson and link between ESL students and the rest of the school."

Dedicated teachers learn to cope with the stresses and other disadvantages, or don't even regard them as such. One education association has summed up the positives and negatives this way: "Teachers do not make much money, but their jobs are usually stable and secure. Teachers spend long hours outside the classroom making preparation . . . working with faculty committees . . . , but these undertakings contribute to the teachers' effectiveness in the classroom and help them to become valued and responsible citizens of the community. Teachers live in a goldfish bowl of community attention and gossip, but they have many pleasant social contacts . . . . Teaching is monotonous work for some, but for others, it is highly individual, creative, and responsible. Teaching is hard work, but it is work that makes a difference in the lives of [students] and ultimately in the future of the nation."

## ESL/EFL Earnings

Although teaching is still one of the lowest-paid professions, salaries and benefits for TESOLers, especially those working overseas, can be higher. Pay and benefits do, however, vary from region to region and employer to employer. ESL pay scales in the United States are usually competitive with other teachers' salaries. Jobs overseas in areas that involve more "hardship" to Americans, such as the Middle East, typically offer higher wages and more special allowances. In such a setting, you would probably receive free housing and furniture, free travel, free medical care, and a bonus at the end of your contract. In poorer countries or in countries where the lifestyle is more compatible with what Americans are used to, salaries are generally lower. However, when you work overseas and meet certain requirements, such as the length of time spent out of the United States, you will not be required to pay U.S. income tax.

Some U.S.-based TESL situations offer the attractive bonus of job security. In four out of five states, ESL teachers working within the public school system are protected by tenure laws stating that a teacher cannot be fired without good cause. Incompetence is basis for dismissal, but a personality conflict with the principal is not.

**Deciding Your Specialty**    In addition to deciding the job setting and the age and proficiency level of students with whom you prefer to work, you can opt to train for a specialty. While it is important for you as an ESL/EFL teacher to be a generalist, to have a solid background in every aspect of the field, it can also be helpful to your career to have more intensive training and experience in one or more areas.

What follows is a listing of the eighteen interest sections TESOL recognizes as concerns within the profession. These sections provide a focus for individual members' specializations. Membership in TESOL automatically offers affiliation with at least three of these interest sections. They are:

> Applied Linguistics
>
> Computer-Assisted Language Learning
>
> English as a Foreign Language
>
> English for Specific Purposes
>
> ESL in Bilingual Education
>
> ESL in Higher Education
>
> ESL in Secondary Education
>
> ESOL in Adult Education
>
> ESOL in Elementary Education
>
> Intensive English Programs
>
> International Teaching Assistants
>
> Materials Writers
>
> Program Administration
>
> Refugee Concerns
>
> Research
>
> Teacher Education
>
> Teaching English to Deaf Students
>
> Video

**Finding Your Overseas EFL Job**    Searching on-line TESOL databases, scanning advertisements in the *Chronicle of Higher Education* and the *Times Educational Supplement* (based in the United Kingdom), attending national and regional conferences where employers recruit, registering with TESOL's job bank, and word of mouth are all excellent ways to locate work.

Registering with a reputable employment agency is another option. International Schools Services (ISS) is an employment agency for teachers and related school personnel. Many other legitimate private employment agencies deal exclusively with teaching and related positions. As a job seeker you will usually be asked to fill out an application; provide several copies of your résumé, diplomas/credentials, and letters of reference; and state preferred geographical locations. You will also be asked to pay a registration/service fee. When signing up with an agency, it is best to go with an organization whose reputation is familiar to you. There are many fly-by-night employment agencies to watch out for. Some of the warning signs are:

- Their fees are exorbitant.

- They insist you fly to their office at your own expense.

- They inform you of just the right job opening and ask you to pay a deposit in "good faith" to hold the job for you.

- They make unreasonable claims, such as promising a woman an EFL position in a private company in Saudi Arabia. (Women are restricted to a few particular job settings in Saudi Arabia.)

You can also contact institutions directly. Institutions, particularly smaller ones overseas, do not always advertise their openings in the United States or through the usual channels. If you hope to work in a particular country or would like to apply to a particular institution, a direct approach can be advantageous.

Your library can help you with listings of domestic and overseas schools, universities, and language centers. For overseas institutions, you can also write or telephone a specific country's embassy in Washington, D.C., and ask for its educational/cultural affairs office. Often the officer in charge of that department also plays some role in the recruitment procedure and will know of any openings in his or her home country.

Traveling overseas "on spec" is the least advised method of finding a job. Some intrepid TESOLers have traveled to their location of choice hoping to find employment upon arrival and have succeeded. In some countries, such as Japan or Spain, on-spec candidates can secure part-time teaching postitions in local language schools or find individual students to tutor privately. But it's a risky proposition. More and more language schools seek professional candidates through the normal channels, and if your travel and living expenses depend upon finding employment, you could find yourself a long way from home without funds.

There are also a few other disadvantages to this method. Many employers who hire staff from the United States or United Kingdom expect to pay for airfare, accommodations, and other expenses such as baggage and settling-in allowances. By arriving unannounced on an employer's doorstep, you might be shortchanging yourself an attractive salary and benefits package. In addition, in some countries work visas can only be obtained when the candidate is outside the country. You could arrive, find a job, then discover that you have to leave again to satisfy work and immigration regulations. Finally, some countries, such as the Persian Gulf states, will deny you entry unless you have a sponsor (an employer) in advance.

# FIRSTHAND ACCOUNTS

## Mary Alice Murphy
## French Instuctor

Mary Alice Murphy has taught French off and on for thirty-three years. She's worked at two universities, University of Wyoming in Laramie and Western New Mexico University in Silver City, and Montgomery College, a community college in The Woodlands, Texas. She earned her bachelor's degree in Spanish then switched to French for her master's degree.

**Getting Started**

"I've always loved words, in any language. The linguistics of how languages are related fascinates me, so that's what I studied. In high school I took two years of Latin and two of Spanish. I found that I had a talent for picking up languages (even dead ones!) and decided to major in Spanish at college. My minor was French. But I soon discovered that French came to me more easily than Spanish, so I decided to continue my schooling by getting a master's degree in French with a specialty in French linguistics. I enjoy reading literature in French, but I much prefer delving into the nuances and origins of the language itself rather than trying to analyze an author and his or her reasons for writing such-and-such a work.

"When I graduated with a master's in the late 1960s, I looked for a job teaching at a small college or university. The acting head of the Department of Romance and Classical Languages at the University of Wyoming interviewed me by phone, and I landed a job as Instructor of French—a job not requiring a Ph.D. at the time. So I moved from warm Texas to cold Laramie and almost froze the first year, but I loved it.

"I taught twelve credit hours of classes each semester, including first- and second-year French, phonetics, and scientific French for graduate students. The latter was probably my favorite because these graduate students, mostly in the sciences, were motivated to learn enough French to be able to read French articles about their specialties. Most of my students in the undergraduate classes were traditional students who had come straight from high school into college. I had twelve to fourteen contact hours with the students per week for approximately fifteen to eighteen weeks each semester: September to December and January to May. The department also required at least four hours of office hours each week so that students had access to their professors. I generally planned my office hours for right before and immediately following class. The year that I had our firstborn daughter, I arranged my classes and office hours for Monday, Wednesday, and Friday only, so that my other days were free for me to be a mother.

"Following four and a half years of being an instructor, I resigned to become a full-time mom and part-time volunteer. Because my husband's job allowed us to live in foreign countries, I continued honing my teaching skills by volunteering to teach English to the women of the countries in which we lived. I also taught conversational English to a group of expatriate Frenchwomen for about four years. One year I held a joint French/English conversational group between English speakers and French speakers, theoretically alternating languages each week. We had fun, but we didn't always stick to the language of the day. I got some great recipes out of the encounter, though."

## What the Work Is Like

"At the University of Wyoming, the students were traditional students, most having just graduated from high school. At Montgomery College, most of my students were older, such as women going back to school after they had raised their families. In New Mexico's continuing education department, the students vary—from a gal whose son was marrying a Belgian girl and she wanted to be able to communicate with the family, to a retired vice president of Exxon who wanted to keep up his French skills.

"I love teaching. The one to three hours that a class may last is fairly relaxed—at least from my point of view. Repetition of phrases is probably boring for the students, but they need it to instill the correct pronunciations and phrasings into their minds. A continuing ed class will last approximately two and a half to three hours, with a fifteen-minute break. Students reading aloud, discussion of grammar points from me, answering questions, repetitions (repeat after me), and short, extemporaneous conversations fill up most of the class time.

"I recently moved to Silver City, New Mexico, and applied for a job at the local university here. Although the head of the foreign language department would like to get French into the curriculum, he hasn't been able to convince the vice president of its worth. So I'll be teaching continuing education classes for awhile."

## Upsides and Downsides

"I enjoyed my continuing ed classes at the community college the most because the students were very motivated—for many different reasons, from wanting to travel to simply wanting to improve their skills in the French language. For me it was wonderful, no papers to grade, no grades to keep—simply the joy of teaching French. We followed the book *Barron's Learning French the Fast and Fun Way*, but I added exercises that I made up and encouraged extemporaneous conversations about the topic of the chapter.

"I like imparting my love of French to students. I love seeing students progress from no French skills to being able to carry on a simple conversation. Downsides for me are the students who aren't motivated, who have no ear for language, and so butcher the pronunciations. I'm not real fond of grading papers, although I enjoy creating challenging exams!"

## Salaries

"In the late 1960s and early 1970s I earned between $6,600 and $7,000 a year for teaching a full load of twelve credit hours. When I resumed a paying teaching job as an adjunct professor (meaning I taught only one curriculum class and was not eligible for any benefits) in the mid-1990s at the community college, I was paid $1,800 per semester for four-and-a-half contact hours per week, plus office hours. It came to about $17 an hour, not much more than I had made per hour twenty-five years before. The only benefits that I could detect were sharing an office with other adjunct professors and an E-mail address at the college.

"When the department at the community college hired a full-time Ph.D. professor to teach French and Spanish, I began teaching a continuing education course in conversational French. The class met for three hours one night a week for eight weeks. Some of my students stayed with me from French I all the way through French V. I was paid a flat $15 an hour."

**Advice from Mary Alice Murphy**

"You better love it because you won't make much money at it. A person should be outgoing and perhaps a ham at heart with some acting skills. For university-level jobs you need at least a master's degree for smaller schools and a Ph.D. for larger universities. I feel it is absolutely mandatory to live in a French-speaking country for at least several months to become totally fluent in the language and to really absorb the nuances of the language."

## Todd Schuett
## EFL Instructor

Todd Schuett worked at several different universities in Japan from 1995 to 1999. He earned his M.A. in religious studies at the University of Chicago Divinity School. (He is currently working in Norway as a translator. Turn to Chapter 4 to see his firsthand account.)

**Getting Started**

"I was attracted to teaching English in Japan because I was attracted to Japan and Japanese Buddhism. The work was a sideline, initially. I got my first teaching assignment in Japan by writing to the dean of faculty (my former college adviser) and asking for a job. The school was a branch campus of my alma mater.

"A graduate degree is required to teach English in a college or university in Japan. For part-time work, Japanese universities don't care if the degree is in a field other than English (any of the liberal arts), though the bigger and better universities require prior teaching experience and some knowledge of Japanese. For a full-time, tenured position, a Ph.D. still isn't required, but publications, research, teaching experience, and Japanese proficiency become increasingly important.

"I've studied Spanish, Greek, French, Japanese, and Norwegian. I claim moderate proficiency only in Japanese and Norwegian. The others I've forgotten. I studied Japanese and Norwegian at language schools in Japan and Norway, respectively. Living in the culture from which a language has grown is essential, in my opinion, for learning a language."

**What the Work Is Like**   "Teaching English at a Japanese university is challenging. English classes are required—which means almost no one wants to be there. While the students have had six years of English language education prior to university, they can only read and translate English to Japanese. And as these students are usually passive learners, they are reluctant to speak more than one word at a time, if at all.

"Western education tends to be Socratic; teachers and students often engage in a volley of questions and answers. Eastern education tends to be more Confucian; teachers assign students material to memorize. This presents an enormous challenge to Western-educated instructors. Volumes have been written on English teaching techniques for Japanese students, and the more dedicated instructors swap ideas and materials between classes. Industrious and enterprising instructors turn their materials into textbooks. All of this is to say that the work is challenging, if you take it seriously and want to do it well. But I have known instructors who only show their students movies in class and then ask them to write a few sentences about each in a journal. They must have based grades on attendance.

"I taught twelve to seventeen classes each semester. That's really too many classes and students to handle well. At the same time, that's the number you need to get a work visa (part-time university teachers can get a self-sponsorship visa if they have enough work to support themselves).

"In some respects, teaching English in Japan is much like teaching anywhere—except that there are rarely discipline problems. The universities generally don't like failure, so there's pressure to go easy on the students."

**Upsides and Downsides**   "The Japanese people are what I liked most. They are gracious as well as very inquisitive. They have a high regard and respect for education. And the culture is unique and intrinsically interesting. But what I liked the least was also the Japanese. Sometimes, it was all I could do to stop from screaming in class, 'Speak! Someone, please speak!'

"Some people don't adjust well to living in Japan. The living quarters are very small, the cities are crowded and noisy, and neighborhood streets have no sidewalks, which means you have to dodge cars and bikes while you're walking. There's also the fact that you can feel very isolated living in a country as foreign as Japan. It's necessary, therefore, to have the proper attitude before you go there. Understand that living there will be difficult and a lot will be incomprehensible at first. Visit large bookstores to find the English language publications that list jobs, activities, and hangouts for foreigners. For Osaka/Kobe/Kyoto, the magazines *Kansai TimeOut* and *Kansai Flea Market* are good sources for information. You should also be able to find them on the Internet.

The point is, don't allow yourself to become socially isolated. I've known people who've become paranoid living in Japan."

### Salaries

"At the U.S. branch campuses, I started out making $40,000 a year in 1993. Four years later, when the school closed, I was making more than $50,000. I was promoted during that time. The part-time Japanese university work was a different story. Classes meet only once a week for ninety minutes. Instructors are paid between $250 and $400 per class, per month, for twelve months. Most universities work with their part-time instructors' schedules, understanding that they often teach at different universities each day. It's possible, therefore, to teach two to four classes every day of the week. The first year teaching part-time in Japanese universities, I got twelve classes. The next year, seventeen. Some people take on more than twenty classes if they can find night classes—three to four classes each day and one or more each night.

"There are no benefits or bonuses included with the salary. However, the greatest part about working part-time for a Japanese university is that you aren't required to do anything except teach. That means no committees and all the extra work usually involved with that. Your first day at work is the first day of the semester and your last day is the last day of the semester. Once you've turned your grades in, you're on vacation.

"As far as vacations go, a Japanese semester is only twelve to fifteen weeks long, and there are only two semesters a year. That means each year you get two vacation periods, each lasting two to three months. And you get paid during that time, too."

### Advice from Todd Schuett

"If you have a graduate degree, go to Japan (Tokyo, Osaka, or Kyoto) and start teaching English in a language school. With a full-time job, you'll get a one-year working visa. During that first year, join JALT (Japanese Association of Language Teachers) and attend all of their meetings and conferences. You'll find out about jobs and meet the university instructors.

"The academic year starts in April. Universities start looking for faculty in the fall, but vacancies come up as late as February and even April. Faculty can suddenly decide to leave Japan. Each year large universities need several new part-time English instructors, but you'll never get an interview, let alone an assignment without first knowing someone at the university (or knowing someone who knows someone).

"Friendly, positive thirty- to forty-year-old people tend to get the most work. Wearing a suit to the interview is necessary. Bring your diplomas (the originals). A master's degree in ESL will open doors, as will Cambridge certification. But the old saying 'It's not what you know but who you know' is doubly true in Japan."

## FOR MORE INFORMATION

Information on licensure or certification requirements and approved teacher training institutions is available from local school systems and state departments of education.

Information on teachers' unions and education-related issues may be obtained from:

American Federation of Teachers
555 New Jersey Avenue NW
Washington, DC 20001

National Education Association
1201 Sixteenth Street NW
Washington, DC 20036

A list of institutions with accredited teacher education programs can be obtained from:

National Council for Accreditation of Teacher Education
2010 Massachusetts Avenue NW, Suite 500
Washington, DC 20036
www.ncate.org

For information on national teacher certification, contact:

National Board for Professional Teaching Standards
26555 Evergreen Road, Suite 400
Southfield, MI 48076
www.nbpts.org

For information on alternative certification programs, contact:

ERIC Clearinghouse on Teacher Education
1307 New York Avenue NW
Washington, DC 20005-4701

For information on teaching English to speakers of other languages, contact:

Teachers of English to Speakers of Other Languages, Inc. (TESOL)
700 South Washington Street, Suite 200
Alexandria, VA 22314
www.tesol.edu

The American Association for Applied Linguistics (AAAL) is a professional organization of scholars who are interested in and actively contribute to the multidisciplinary field of applied linguistics. AAAL members promote principled approaches to language-related concerns, including language education, acquisition and loss, bilingualism, discourse analysis, literacy, rhetoric and stylistics, language for special purposes, psycholinguistics, second and foreign language pedagogy, language assessment, and language policy and planning. Contact them at:

The American Association for Applied Linguistics
P.O. Box 21686
Eagan, MN 55121-0686
www.aaal.org

American Association of Language Specialists
1000 Connecticut Avenue NW, Suite 9
Washington, DC 20036

The American Council on the Teaching of Foreign Languages (ACTFL) is a national organization dedicated to the improvement and expansion of the teaching and learning of all languages at all levels of instruction. ACTFL is an individual membership organization of more than seven thousand foreign language educators and administrators from elementary through graduate education, as well as government and industry.

American Council on the Teaching of Foreign Languages
6 Executive Plaza
Yonkers, NY 10701
www.actfl.org

Founded in 1883, the Modern Language Association provides opportunities for its members to share their scholarly findings and teaching experiences with colleagues and to discuss trends in the academy. MLA members host an annual convention and other meetings, work with related organizations, and sustain one of the finest publishing programs in the humanities. For more than one hundred years, members have worked to strengthen the study and teaching of language and literature. Contact them at:

Modern Language Association (MLA)
10 Astor Place
New York, NY 10003-6981
212-475-9500
212-477-9863 (fax)
www.mla.org

National Association for Bilingual Education (NABE) is a national organization exclusively concerned with the education of language-minority students in American schools. Contact them at:

National Association for Bilingual Education
1220 L Street NW, Suite 605
Washington, DC 20005-4018
www.nabe.org

The National Clearinghouse for Bilingual Education (NCBE) is funded by the U.S. Department of Education's Office of Bilingual Education and Minority Languages Affairs (OBEMLA) to collect, analyze, and disseminate information relating to the effective education of linguistically and culturally diverse learners in the United States.

NCBE provides information through its website and produces a biweekly news bulletin, *Newsline*, and manages a topical electronic discussion group, NCBE Roundtable. As part of the U.S. Department of Education's technical assistance and information network, NCBE works with other service providers to provide access to high-quality information to help states and local school districts develop programs and implement strategies for helping all students work toward high academic standards.

NCBE is operated by George Washington University, Graduate School of Education and Human Development. Send mail to:

NCBE
George Washington University
Center for the Study of Language and Education
2011 Eye Street NW, Suite 200
Washington, DC 20006
www.ncbe.gwu.edu

These other organizations and websites are also worth contacting:

American Association of Teachers of Arabic: Encourages communication and cooperation among teachers of Arabic and promotes study, criticism, research, and instruction in Arabic language, linguistics, and literature.

American Association of Teachers of Arabic (AATA)
Department of Modern Languages and Literatures
College of William and Mary
Williamsburg, VA 23187-8795
757-221-3145
757-221-3637 (fax)
www.wm.edu/aata

Association of Departments of Foreign Languages, a Division of MLA
www.adfl.org

Center for Advanced Research on Language Acquisition
619 Heller Hall
271 Nineteenth Avenue S
Minneapolis, MN 55455
612-626-8600
612-624-7514 (fax)

Center for Applied Linguistics
4646 Fortieth Street NW
Washington, DC 20016-1859
202-362-0700
202-362-3740 (fax)
www.cal.org

ERIC Clearinghouse on Languages and Linguistics
www.cal.org/ericcll
    The ERIC Clearinghouse on Languages and Linguistics is operated by the
Center for Applied Linguistics and funded by the U.S. Department of Education, Office of Educational Research and Improvement, National Library of
Education.

Internet Resources for Language Teachers and Learners
www.hull.ac.uk/cti/langsite.htm

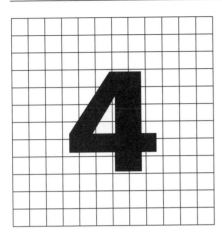

# INTERPRETING, TRANSLATING, EDITING, AND WRITING

People who use their knowledge of other languages as a primary skill in their jobs most often work as interpreters or translators. Editing and writing in a foreign language are other areas in which bilingual individuals use language as a primary career skill.

But just because an individual is bilingual doesn't mean that these careers are shoe-ins. For example, a surprising number of bilingual people cannot listen to a speech or a statement in one language and then repeat clearly and precisely in another language the ideas that have just been presented. Knowing another language is not enough. Simultaneous interpreting requires the additional skill of listening intently to one language while speaking another language at the same time.

Interpretation and translation are demanding disciplines. Not everyone has an aptitude for them, and those who do must work hard to acquire the necessary education.

## INTERPRETING

An interpreter conveys into another language the spoken words of, for example, politicians, businesspeople, celebrities, or athletes. Instant reactions, a fine memory, and stamina are just as important as expertise in languages.

There are different types of interpreting: escort interpreting, conference interpreting, business interpreting, and court interpreting. All require expertise in the field in which the interpreter is hired. An interpreter may need to understand the workings of the European Commission, the Social Security system, or immigration legislation, for example. Other personal skills, such as negotiating and the ability to work under stress, are also essential.

## Escort Interpreting

Escort interpreters accompany and interpret for visiting delegations or individuals usually in informal situations. There are more escort interpreters than conference interpreters because more languages are in demand for escort interpreting. The temporary assignments in this field are uncertain and sporadic, so escort interpreting should not be viewed as a permanent career or as a sole means of livelihood. And while the work is extremely interesting and educational and as a contribution to international understanding can be most rewarding, most people eventually tire of the frequent and even constant travel involved.

## Conference Interpreting

Conference interpreting usually involves simultaneous transmission through headphones of speeches that would otherwise be unintelligible to the delegates. Conference interpreters form a small, highly paid, elite group and are often freelancers who have acquired a reputation through long apprenticeship.

Conference interpreting is also known as simultaneous or consecutive interpreting, but this is more likely in a social or business setting. The difference between them is that in consecutive interpreting, no equipment is necessary. The interpreter makes notes to recall what is being said and, once the speaker has finished, gives his or her interpretation.

Opportunities in the field of conference interpreting are fairly limited. The United Nations has a staff of some ninety-eight interpreters, all of whom are required to know extremely well at least two and preferably three of the UN conference languages. These languages are Arabic, Chinese, English, French, Russian, and Spanish. The next largest group of interpreters in a national or international organization in the United States (not including the armed forces) is in the State Department. The State Department normally has fifty or so linguists on its interpreting and translating staff, of whom about twenty are primarily interpreters. (For more information on working for the government, turn to Chapter 5.) The World Bank, International Monetary Fund, and Organization of American States also hire a small number of interpreters on a full-time basis in national and international agencies. Vacancies are few and far between, with many applicants applying for each opening.

Virtually the only languages used in international conferences in the United States are English, French, German, Japanese, Portuguese, Russian, and Spanish.

## Business Interpreters

Business interpreters perform essentially the same functions as conference interpreters but work for private concerns.

## Court Interpreters

Court interpreters work in courtrooms, interpreting the proceedings for speakers of languages other than the court-approved language. Sign language experts can also be hired to work in courtrooms to interpret the proceedings for the deaf.

**Freelancing**          The freelance conference interpreting field in the United States is made up of experienced interpreters who compete for the opportunity to interpret at international conferences on scientific, economic, political, and other subjects. Except for the very few best-known and most-experienced interpreters, who are frequently multilingual rather than merely bilingual, freelancing as a conference interpreter is an uncertain occupation.

## TRANSLATING, EDITING, AND WRITING

While interpreting involves spoken words, translation involves written texts. Your focus could be on literary translation, which includes novels and poetry, or nonliterary translation, including scientific, technical, and commercial documents. It is common to hear the term *translation* used loosely to refer to both interpretation and translation, though it more properly refers only to written work.

For the most part, translating is done into the translator's native tongue. Most translator positions require the ability to translate from several foreign languages into English. Some require the ability to edit and/or write in a foreign language at an educated native level. Material could include, for example, advertising copy for ethnic or foreign markets; technical specifications; or diplomatic, informal, or scientific information. Employers could include film production and entertainment media or editors for university and other presses. A broad background of education and experience is required to translate documents on many diverse subjects. All translators have access to dictionaries, lexicons, and even databases.

**Technical Translation**          A major part of the translation field is technical translation. For this work you will need to be expert in the field you are employed in: science, technology, or business, for example. Even in the less-specialized areas, you need more than just an ability to find the right word—you must be able to write authoritatively in English and/or the target language as well.

This area also includes dubbing and subtitling, monitoring the broadcast media, and abstracting. However, few openings exist in these areas even for exceptionally gifted linguists.

**Legal Translation**          Here, law qualifications as well as precise language ability—in both English and the foreign language—are necessary. International law is an important field, and more and more contracts and other legal documents must be accurately translated.

**Literary Translation**

Literary translation forms the basis of most readers' acquaintance with world literature. But full-time literary translators are very rare. This type of work usually goes to creative writers, academics, or others who rely on another source of income for their economic survival.

**Machine Translation**

Translation done by computers and purpose-built machines is still in its infancy and almost always requires an editor to revise the text or even to retranslate parts, especially idiomatic phrases.

As with interpreting, seldom can a translator make his or her living through translating work alone. Assignments are often temporary and sporadic. Jobs can be found through Internet searches or through networking contacts.

## JOB OPPORTUNITIES

A visit to www.nettrade.com.au/shane/sawtrans/links.htm will lead you to a list of links to translating agencies. Your own search will bring you to international companies that have foreign language websites and need their content translated into English, or to English-speaking companies that want to reach a foreign audience.

Public and private libraries also hire or work with translators to translate foreign publications. Some research librarians also need to be skilled in a foreign language.

For those interested in freelancing, creating a Web page for yourself and registering with the various search engines would be a good way to find clients.

For European readers, there are opportunities with the European Commission. People employed by the commission reflect the cultural diversity of the member states of the European Union. Jobs are open only to women and men who are nationals of an EU member state. They must feel at ease in a multicultural and multilingual working environment outside their home country. Entry is mainly by open competition. To be a successful candidate at any level, you will need to show ability, initiative, and motivation. Only candidates with a university degree may apply, and only the very best are hired.

Additional information about careers as translators and interpreters can be obtained from the following addresses:

European Commission
Joint Interpreting and Conference Service
Wetstraat, rue de la Loi, 200
B-1049 Brussels
32/2/296 43 06 (fax)

European Commission
Translation Service
SdT 01
Wetstraat, rue de la Loi, 200
B-1049 Brussels
32/2/295 62 20
32/2/295 65 03 (fax)

## TRAINING

Even those who are self-taught or bi- or multilingual from a young age need additional training for interpreting, translating, editing, or writing in a foreign language. Most universities offer courses and full B.A. programs that lead to a variety of degrees. A bachelor's degree program could be in Russian or French studies, for example, or in international relations or international studies. In addition to specific language courses, other offerings could cover topics such as the following:

Comparative economic systems

Comparative foreign policy

Comparative politics

Conflict and conflict resolution

Contemporary African politics

Cultural anthropology

History

International economics

International law

International organization

International politics

Latin American politics

Political anthropology

Political ideologies

Sociology

Third World politics

Many universities also offer graduate programs in translating and interpreting, with courses covering a wide range—from literary translation theory, discourse analysis, and communication theory to publishing, public relations, and personnel.

To become a competent interpreter, a considerable amount of practical training is required. Depending on the program, students work on acquiring consecutive interpreting skills, memory skills, and note-taking and eventually move into simultaneous interpreting, simulating real-life situations in the booth. For those going into specific fields, such as business or legal interpreting, programs that focus on practical training are helpful but must also offer courses in the particular area, such as finance, law, or information technology.

"When choosing a school," says Patrick Lafferty, a lecturer at Georgetown University, "consider the program's reputation for producing graduates who do well in the profession. Major employers of interpretation or translation services, practicing interpreters and translators, and professional organizations for language-service personnel can be helpful sources of information."

The American Translators Association (ATA) has compiled a list of schools in North America that offer course work in the field. The publication is called *Translator and Interpreter Programs in North America, a Survey*. The contact address is listed at the end of this chapter.

## PERSONAL QUALIFICATIONS

To find out if this field would be a good fit for you, explore the profession by talking with professional interpreters or translators. Search the Internet for local chapters of the professional organizations for interpreters and translators and ask them to provide you with information on meetings in your area. Also consult bulletins, journals, and Web pages on interpretation and translation to locate meetings and conferences on the profession. Check with institutions that offer programs in interpretation and translation; their summer programs dealing with the professional aspects of the field might offer you some good exposure without a full-time commitment.

## FIRSTHAND ACCOUNTS

### Beverly Stafford
### Freelance Translator, Copyeditor, and Proofreader

Beverly Stafford is self-employed and based in Mallorca, Spain. She has a diploma from British Columbia Institute of Technology, Vancouver, in computer programming, with a minor in technical writing.

**Getting Started**

"I did not set out to work as a translator. I considered myself (and still do) first and foremost a writer. However, I have always had a knack for languages, having gone to a French/English bilingual school and having learned Spanish as a teenager, and this led to the translating work.

"I now live in Spain, and when I heard about the then upcoming World University Games, I approached the organizing office for information for an article I was researching. At the same time, I signed up as a volunteer, thinking of helping out with the Canadian team. Instead of that I was offered the job as head of the translations department. At first I looked on it as a way to be involved in an exciting event, but I soon found that I enjoyed the translating more than I had expected to.

"My duties involved working with all of the different departments of the organizing committee. They first had to produce preliminary documentation, describing the proposed procedures to be followed during the games. This was done about a year before the start of the games and included both behind-the-scenes services and the sports' competition procedures. All of this was written in Spanish, and I then had to translate it to English and sometimes French.

"The pressure was enormous on everyone as there were always deadlines, and if the original documents were not ready because of last-minute changes, it could mean that I would have to work through the night to have the English versions done on time. This was an expected part of the job since we were dealing with a once-in-a-lifetime event, and the end of the job was always on the horizon. The World University Games is second only to the Olympics in size and complexity.

"During the year running up to the Games in July 1999, we produced four informational magazines, three service bulletins, one guidebook, and a technical manual for each of the twelve sports. I must have translated hundreds of letters and messages that were constantly flying back and forth among sports experts, participating countries, and visiting dignitaries.

"The best part of the job was definitely just being involved in something that interested me. I have always loved sports, and the type of people who are involved in these events are always dynamic, energetic, and upbeat. There was also the ego part of seeing my work printed and distributed around the world. My last project for the Games was the official book. I actually wrote most of it and did the translation myself. It is a three-hundred-fifty-page account of the Games with pictures and results tables."

**What the Work Is Like**

"When my contract finally came to an end, I decided to look into continuing with the translating work. I had previously worked from home as a freelance writer and was anxious to get back into my home office on a full-time basis. I have since taken out a business license as a translator and have been fortunate to land a few good, steady clients. I regularly translate for the University Games governing body, which is based in Brussels, Belgium. I also handle the publications and translations for the Palma City Hall sports section for any international sports events. Through people I met at the Games last July, I have since translated a one-hundred-thousand-word book on the history of European basketball, and a few months ago I translated a movie script. I could register with local translating agencies, but since that would probably involve things like legal documents and tourism, I am not that keen. I find I would rather concentrate on sports topics, and I can pick up that type of work directly."

**Salaries**

"For the Games, I was on a standard forty-hour-a-week salary, earning about $35,000 a year, and we received a two-months salary bonus and six weeks paid holiday after the Games. But none of us was there for the money.

"As a freelance translator, I charge by the word. Agencies typically charge around fourteen cents per word here in Spain. They pay translators nine cents, so I charge ten or eleven. My average speed works out that I earn around $60 to $70 per hour. My selling point is the specialized knowledge I have gained in the sports field. I have loads of reference books on sports regulations, procedures, etcetera, and eleven dictionaries. I can also use the Internet to research any specific points as needed."

**Advice from Beverly Stafford**

"Translating for a specific event can mean being at the right place at the right time. My approach of going in as a volunteer worked in this case. When an event such as a world trade fair, an expo, the Olympics, an international sports championship, etcetera, is announced, find out who is organizing it (often a branch of a city hall) and send in a letter of introduction and your résumé. Conference organizers and universities could also be good sources of translating work.

"Top writing skills are the most important asset for a translator. Just being able to speak English because you were born in the States is not enough. You must be able to express ideas and concepts as clearly and briefly as possible. It is nearly always necessary to adapt ideas and change things around so that they make sense in the target language. A very high comprehension of the source language is necessary, especially if slang and catchy phrases are involved. Most people translate into their native language.

"I have heard concerns expressed about computer translating programs taking over the market. I think this is still a long way off. The complexities involved are more than a machine can handle. For example, in Spanish, for 'hace sol,' a machine would translate it literally to 'makes sun.' But in English we would say 'it is sunny.'

"If you can, I think it is a good idea to specialize in something that you know about and that interests you. The more you know about something, the faster you can translate and the more you can earn.

"It is also very important to have top computer skills. An inside-out knowledge of word processing programs is essential. With all the shortcuts like macros, automatic correction, not to mention word counts, you can cut down the time you spend typing considerably. I use Word 97 because it is so widely used, though I just bought a secondhand Mac because so many printers and designers use Mac, and I don't want to be shut out of some opportunities.

"With the Internet and E-mail, it is no longer necessary to be in the same place as your client. Documents can just as easily be sent around the world as across town, so an E-mail address is a definite plus, and even a Web page could be used to promote your service and display your work.

"To sum up, if you are a native English speaker living in a foreign country and really love to work with words, translating can be a lucrative and interesting career option. If you have ever picked up a brochure or even a restaurant menu that gave you a pain in the head because it was badly translated into English, then you already know where to find clients."

## Todd Schuett
## Translator

After teaching EFL in Japan (see his firsthand account in Chapter 3), Todd Schuett moved to Norway and now works as a reporter and translator for *The Norway Post*, an on-line newspaper based in Oslo.

**Getting Started**

"When I first moved to Norway, I surfed the Web looking for job opportunities. I came across *The Norway Post*, which was just starting up. Despite the fact that virtually all Norwegians can speak, or at least understand, English, there is very little English-language information available in Norway, about Norway—unless you're interested in tourist information. *The Norway Post*, therefore, was a welcome find.

"Initially I didn't think about translating for *The Norway Post*. It was my wife (who is Norwegian) who suggested I contact them, which I did, citing editorial experience and previous publications, including a small newspaper. I thought I could do some reporting, perhaps proofreading or copyediting for them. The editor responded favorably to my résumé and asked me to translate an article written in Norwegian. I'd studied Norwegian for only a few months at the time, so my wife and I cotranslated the article. He found it acceptable, and I've been translating two long articles per week ever since."

**What the Work Is Like**

"*The Norway Post* is found only on the Internet. There is no business office. Therefore, I work at home. My editor E-mails assignments to me, and I E-mail the translations to him when I'm finished. I'm often given a deadline, and if I go on vacation, I double-up on the work before I leave.

"It's solitary, detailed work that requires a lot of creative thinking. Translating from Norwegian into colloquial English requires the translator to have not only a strong grasp of the foreign language but also excellent written English skills. If you know the foreign language but possess poor written English skills, the translation comes out sounding flat, wooden, or simply bad."

**Upsides and Downsides**

"I like that I can work at home, at any time of the day or night. There's a lot of freedom in that. In addition, translating has advanced my Norwegian language skills significantly. What I like the least is the isolation. I have only 'virtual' coworkers. My employers held an annual Christmas dinner at a nice restaurant in downtown Oslo. When I got to the restaurant, I had to ask where the *Norway*

*Post* guests were seated and was lead to a table of strangers. It was an awkward moment for all of us."

**Salaries**

"I only translate two to three hours a week, and I'm paid 2,000 kroner a month (about $250). It's not much, but then, I don't work much.

"Perks? There's the fact that I can see my name 'in print' on the computer screen. Also, I've started writing original feature articles for them, and I'll be helping with a new advertising venture."

**Advice from Todd Schuett**

"For translating from the written word to the written word, you have to be efficient and detail-oriented. If you have trouble working alone, under a deadline, or need the presence of other people for motivation, you won't enjoy yourself.

"If you are fluent in a foreign language, I would suggest approaching companies, publications, and institutions that need translators. It's better if they are involved in something that interests you.

"I got into this work with no prior experience. I think it's the sort of thing where, if you can deliver the goods, you've got the job. Companies will want to test prospective translators with little or no experience. If you're offered a test, don't hesitate to take it. Finish the assignment promptly and present it to them with confidence."

## FOR MORE INFORMATION

American Literary Translators' Association (ALTA)
University of Texas at Dallas
MC35, Box 830688
Richardson, TX 75083-0688
www.utdallas.edu

American Society of Interpreters
P.O. Box 9603
Washington, DC 20036

American Translators Association
109 Croton Avenue
Ossining, NY 10562

# CAREERS IN GOVERNMENT

The government is the largest employer in the United States, with more than 3 million workers throughout more than one hundred agencies, departments, boards, bureaus, and commissions. The need for professionals with foreign language skills extends through many of these departments and agencies. Some positions require a language as the primary skill; others, as a secondary skill. Here is a partial list of potential job titles:

Air Safety Investigator
Border Patrol Agent
Customs Inspector
Equal Employment Opportunity
   Specialist
Foreign Affairs Specialist
Foreign Agricultural Affairs
   Specialist
Foreign Service Officer/Diplomat

Intelligence Specialist
International Relations Specialist
Interpreter
Linguist
Public Affairs Specialist
Teacher
Trade Specialist
Translator
U.S. Census Taker

Federal workers can be posted in the United States or overseas, although most positions requiring language skills are abroad. Federal agencies that employ individuals overseas include, but are not limited to, the following:

Agency for International
   Development
Department of Agriculture
Department of the Air Force
Department of the Army
Department of Commerce

Department of Defense
Department of the Navy
Department of State
Drug Enforcement Agency
Peace Corps
U.S. Information Agency

## GETTING HIRED

The federal government has technical, administrative, and supervisory employment opportunities overseas. These positions are usually in the competitive civil service, and as vacancies occur, they are filled in most cases by transferring career federal employees from the United States. Only when federal employees are not available for transfer overseas and qualified United States citizens cannot be recruited locally are these vacancies filled through the open examination process. Individuals may also apply directly to federal agencies for excepted service positions, such as attaché office clerk-translator, translator, interpreter, and Foreign Service and Department of State positions.

## EXCEPTED SERVICE AGENCIES

Most federal government civilian positions are part of the civil service. To obtain a federal job, you must vie with other applicants in open competition. Some agencies are excluded from these procedures. These agencies, called excepted service agencies, have their own hiring system that establishes the evaluation criteria they use to fill their internal vacancies.

If you are interested in employment with an excepted service agency, contact that agency directly. The U.S. Office of Personnel Management does not provide application forms or information on jobs in excepted service agencies or organizations.

## THE FEDERAL JOB SEARCH AND APPLICATION FORM

USAJOBS is the official website for government jobs and employment information. It can be accessed at www.usajobs.opm.gov.

USAJOBS provides easily accessible federal employment information, worldwide job vacancy information, employment information fact sheets, and job applications and forms, and has on-line résumé development and electronic transmission capabilities. In many instances, job seekers can apply for positions on-line.

USAJOBS is updated every business day from a database of more than 7,500 worldwide job opportunities. It is available in a variety of formats, ensuring access for customers with differing physical and technological capabilities. It is convenient, user friendly, accessible through computer or telephone, and available twenty-four hours a day, seven days a week.

Once you have found an opportunity that interests you, you will need more information on the specific opportunity and appropriate application forms. Use USAJOBS to obtain a copy of the vacancy announcement, which will answer most of the questions you may have. For example: deadlines for applications, specific duties of the position, whether a written test is required, educational requirements, duty location, salary, and so on.

You may apply for most jobs with a résumé or the Optional Application for Federal Employment (OF-612), or any written format you choose. For jobs that are unique or filled through automated procedures, you may be given special forms and/or instructions in the job announcement. Although the federal government does not require a standard application form for most jobs, certain information is needed to evaluate your qualifications. If you decide to submit any format other than the OF-612 (e.g., a résumé), the following information must be included:

- **Job information**—Announcement number, title, and grade.

- **Personal information**—Full name, mailing address (with zip code), day and evening phone numbers (with area code), social security number, country of citizenship, veterans' preference, reinstatement eligibility, highest federal civilian grade held.

- **Education**—High school name, city and state, colleges or universities (name, city, and state), majors, and type and year of any degrees received (if no degree, show total credits earned and indicate whether semester or quarter hours).

- **Work experience**—Job title, duties and accomplishments, employer's name and address, supervisor's name and phone number, starting and ending dates (month and year), hours per week, salary. Indicate whether your current supervisor may be contacted. Prepare a separate entry for each job.

- **Other qualifications**—Job-related training courses (title and year); job-related skills; job-related certificates and licenses; job-related honors, awards, and special accomplishments.

## FEDERAL JOB SCAMS

Information on job vacancies with the federal government and the U.S. Postal Service is provided free of charge. However, many Americans are victimized by scam artists selling information about federal job opportunities. These scam artists place classified advertisements in newspapers and periodicals offering—for a fee—to help job seekers locate and apply for federal jobs. Some companies go so far as to use names that imply affiliation with the federal government, such as the "U.S. Agency for Career Advancement" or "Postal Employment Service."

The U.S. Office of Personnel Management's Federal Employment Information System is the official source for employment information and contains federal job listings as well as some state, local government, and private-sector listings. Information about federal job opportunities is available to the public free of charge, with the exception of local phone company charges for long-distance calls. Federal agencies and the postal service never charge for applications, sell study guides for examinations, or guarantee that you will be hired. If an examination is required, the agency administering the examination typically offers free sample questions to applicants scheduled for the examination.

The Federal Trade Commission and the U.S. Office of Personnel Management urge consumers to protect themselves against job scams. Beware of advertisements or sales pitches containing the following:

- An implied affiliation with the federal government, a guarantee of high test scores or jobs, references to "hidden" or unadvertised job vacancies, or claims that "no experience is necessary."

- Referrals to a toll-free phone number. Often in these cases, an operator encourages you to buy a "valuable" booklet containing job listings, practice test questions, and tips for entrance examinations. These materials may be inaccurate, unnecessary, or available at no charge from the hiring agency.

- Toll-free numbers that direct you to pay-per-call numbers for more information. Under federal law, any solicitations for pay-per-call numbers must contain full disclosures about cost. The solicitation must make clear if there is or is not an affiliation with the federal government. You must have a chance to hang up before you incur any charges.

If you have concerns about an employment advertisement or a company offering employment services, you may contact the following:

Federal Trade Commission, 202-326-3128

Postal Crime Hotline, U.S. Postal Inspection Service, 800-654-8896 (available 24 hours a day)

National Fraud Information Center (a project of the National Consumers League), 800-876-7060 (weekdays, 9:00 A.M. to 5:00 P.M. Eastern Standard Time) or www.fraud.org

Your state attorney general or local Better Business Bureau

## QUALIFICATIONS FOR WORKING OVERSEAS

The qualification requirements for those seeking overseas employment are similar to those established for positions in the United States. Applicants may be required to meet certain additional or higher standards. For example, foreign language capability, while not required in all federal jobs overseas, would obviously be a valuable qualification. Of course, each position has different requirements, such as degrees earned, years of experience in a certain field, and so on. These qualifications are listed with the posted job announcements.

## SALARIES OVERSEAS

Overseas white-collar employees are paid the same base salaries as federal employees in the continental United States. Where warranted by conditions at the post, employees may receive a post differential or cost of living allowance. In foreign areas, the wages of blue-collar employees are based on continental United States rates and, in some cases, a post differential or cost of living allowance.

Most federal jobs are given a general schedule (GS) ranking. This is the breakdown of pay for the year 2000:

| | | | | | |
|---|---|---|---|---|---|
| GS-1 | $13,870 | GS-6 | $23,820 | GS-11 | $39,178 |
| GS-2 | $15,594 | GS-7 | $26,470 | GS-12 | $46,955 |
| GS-3 | $17,015 | GS-8 | $29,315 | GS-13 | $55,837 |
| GS-4 | $19,100 | GS-9 | $32,380 | GS-14 | $65,983 |
| GS-5 | $21,370 | GS-10 | $35,658 | GS-15 | $77,614 |

GS pay is adjusted geographically, and the majority of jobs pay a higher salary. When locality payments are included, pay rates in the continental United States are 6.78 to 15.01 percent higher. Pay rates outside the continental United States are 10 to 25 percent higher. Also, certain hard-to-fill jobs, usually in the scientific, technical, and medical fields, may have higher starting salaries. Exact pay information is provided on actual position vacancy announcements.

To view the 2000 "locality pay charts"—salaries per state—go to this Web address: www.opm.gov/oca/2000tbls/GSannual/index.htm.

Applying for a federal job is covered later in this chapter.

## VOCATIONAL OPPORTUNITIES FOR LINGUISTS

**Interpreting**

U.S. government interpreters must be exceptionally fluent in the languages they interpret, and their speech must be free of any objectionable accent or impediment. They must have a genuine aptitude for interpreting, which is by no means synonymous with being bilingual. (See Chapter 4 for more information on interpreting careers.) At the very least, the aspiring interpreter should be well and broadly educated and almost bilingual, with a fairly long period of residence abroad considered indispensable. Practical experience in several specialized fields is helpful, and a knowledge of political science and economics is important.

**Translating**

Translators of written documents are in greater demand than interpreters in both national and international agencies as well as in private industry. The United Nations has 250 to 300 translators; the State Department has about one-tenth that number; most international agencies and some U.S. agencies have smaller translating staffs.

See Chapter 4 for more information on translating for nongovernment concerns.

**Other Opportunities**

Other vocational opportunities for students of languages exist, such as bilingual secretary or teacher, but the most widespread use of linguistic ability is to supplement other skills and knowledge. The United States Information Agency, for example, uses foreign language announcers and scriptwriters. Other agencies employ analysts in scientific and technical fields, and they may be required to read a foreign language.

In many fields of specialization, the person who knows one or more foreign languages has a distinct advantage in competing for a job and in keeping up with what is going on in his or her field in other parts of the world.

## THE MILITARY

Military personnel are stationed throughout the United States and in many countries around the world. More than a third of military jobs are located in California, Texas, North Carolina, or Virginia. About 258,000 individuals are stationed outside the United States, including those assigned to ships at sea. Over 116,000 of these are stationed in Europe, mainly in Germany, and another 96,000 are assigned to East Asia and the Pacific area, mostly in Japan and the Republic of Korea. In 1999, more than 1.2 million individuals were on active duty in the armed forces—about 445,000 in the army, 272,000 in the navy, 343,000 in the air force, 143,000 in the Marine Corps, and 26,000 in the Coast Guard.

Foreign language skills are not necessary for most military positions, but they come in handy for those posted overseas. Some military officers, especially those people posted overseas at bases or U.S. embassies, would benefit greatly from foreign language proficiency.

The military distinguishes between enlisted and officer careers. Enlisted personnel make up about 85 percent of the armed forces and carry out its fundamental operations in areas such as combat, administration, construction, engineering, health care, and human resources. Officers, who make up the remaining 15 percent, are the leaders of the military. They supervise and manage activities in every occupational specialty in the military.

**Enlisted Occupational Groups**

Administrative careers include a wide variety of positions. The military must keep accurate information for planning and managing its operations, including paper and electronic records on equipment, funds, personnel, supplies, and other property. Enlisted administrative personnel record information, type reports, and maintain files. Personnel may work in a specialized area such as finance, accounting, legal, maintenance, or supply.

Combat specialty occupations refer to enlisted specialties, such as infantry, artillery, and special forces, that operate weapons or execute special missions during combat situations.

Construction occupations in the military involve building or repairing buildings, airfields, bridges, foundations, dams, bunkers, and the electrical and plumbing components of these structures.

Media and public affairs careers include occupations involving the public presentation and interpretation of military information and events. Enlisted media and public affairs personnel take and develop photographs; film, record, and edit audio and video programs; present news and music programs; and produce graphic artwork, drawings, and other visual displays. Other public affairs specialists act as interpreters and translators to convert spoken or written foreign languages into English or other languages.

The military has many engineering, science, and technical occupations that require specific knowledge to operate technical equipment, solve complex problems, or provide and interpret information. Enlisted personnel normally specialize in an area such as information technology, space operations, environmental health and safety, or intelligence. Information technology specialists develop software programs and operate computer systems. Space operations specialists use and repair spacecraft ground control command equipment, including electronic systems that track spacecraft location and operation. Environmental health and safety specialists inspect military facilities and food supplies for the presence of disease, germs, or other conditions hazardous to health and the environment. Intelligence specialists gather and study information using aerial photographs and various types of radar and surveillance systems.

Health care personnel assist medical professionals in treating and providing services for patients. They may work as part of a patient service team in close contact with doctors, dentists, nurses, and physical therapists to provide the necessary support functions within a hospital or clinic. (The Marine Corps employs no medical personnel; medical services are provided by the navy.)

Human resource development specialists recruit and place qualified personnel and provide the training programs necessary to help people perform their jobs effectively.

Recruiting specialists provide information about military careers to young people, parents, schools, and local communities. They explain service employment and training opportunities, pay and benefits, and the nature of service life.

Personnel specialists collect and store information about people's careers in the military, including training, job assignment, promotion, and health information.

Training specialists and instructors provide military personnel with the knowledge needed to perform their jobs.

Machine operator and production careers include occupations that require the operation of industrial equipment, machinery, and tools to fabricate and repair parts for a variety of items and structures.

Protective service personnel enforce military laws and regulations and provide emergency response to natural and man-made disasters.

Support services occupations include subsistence services and occupations that support the morale and well-being of military personnel and their families. For example, food service specialists prepare all types of food in dining halls, hospitals, and ships. Counselors help military personnel and their families overcome social problems. The military also provides chaplains and religious-program specialists to help meet the spiritual needs of its personnel.

Transportation and material handling specialists ensure the safe transport of people and cargo.

Vehicle and machinery mechanics conduct preventive and corrective maintenance on aircraft, automotive, and heavy equipment; heating and cooling systems; marine engines; and power station equipment.

## Officer Occupational Groups

For every enlisted category, there is a category of officer in charge of the specific occupational group.

## Qualifications— Enlisted Personnel

To join the armed services, enlisted personnel must sign a legal agreement called an enlistment contract, which usually involves a commitment to eight years of service. Depending on the terms of the contract, two to six years are spent on active duty and the balance in the reserves. The contract obligates the service to provide the agreed-upon job, rating, pay, cash bonuses for enlistment in certain occupations, medical and other benefits, occupational training, and continuing education. In return, enlisted personnel must serve satisfactorily for the specified period of time.

Requirements for each service vary, but certain qualifications for enlistment are common to all branches. One must be between the ages of seventeen and thirty-five, be a U.S. citizen or immigrant alien holding permanent resident status, have no felony record, and possess a birth certificate. Applicants who are seventeen must have the consent of a parent or legal guardian before entering the service.

Air force enlisted personnel must enter active duty before their twenty-eighth birthday. Applicants must pass a written examination—the Armed Services Vocational Aptitude Battery—and meet certain minimum physical standards for height, weight, vision, and overall health. All branches require high school graduation or its equivalent for certain enlistment options. In 1999, more than nine out of ten volunteers were high school graduates. Single parents are generally ineligible to enlist.

Women are eligible to enter most military specialties. Although many women serve in medical and administrative support positions, women also work as mechanics, missile maintenance technicians, heavy-equipment operators, fighter pilots, and intelligence officers. Only occupations involving direct exposure to combat are excluded.

If you are thinking about enlisting in the military, learn as much as you can about military life before making a decision. This is especially important if you are thinking about making the military a career. Speaking to friends and relatives with military experience is a good idea. Determine what the military can offer you and what it will expect in return. Then talk to a recruiter, who can determine if you qualify for enlistment, explain the various enlistment options, and tell you which military occupational specialties have openings. Bear in mind that the recruiter's job is to recruit promising applicants into military service, so the information he or she gives you is likely to stress the positive aspects of military life in the branch in which the recruiter serves.

Following enlistment, new members of the armed forces undergo recruit training, better known as basic training. Recruit training provides a six- to eleven-week introduction to military life with courses in military skills and protocol. Days and nights are carefully structured and include rigorous physical exercises designed to improve strength and endurance and build unit cohesion. Following basic training, most recruits take additional training at technical schools that prepare them for a particular military occupational specialty. The formal training period generally lasts from ten to twenty weeks.

Many servicepeople get college credit for the technical training they receive on duty, which, combined with off-duty courses, can lead to an associate's degree through community college programs such as the Community College of the Air Force.

**Warrant Officers**

Warrant officers are technical and tactical leaders who specialize in a specific technical area. One group of warrant officers is army aviators. The Army Warrant Officer Corps comprises less than 3 percent of the total army. Although small in size, their level of responsibility is high. They receive extended career opportunities, worldwide leadership assignments, and increased pay and retirement benefits. Selection to attend the Warrant Officer Candidate School is highly competitive and restricted to those with the rank of E-5 or higher (see Table 5.1).

**Officers**

Officer training in the armed forces is provided through the federal service academies (military, naval, air force, and Coast Guard); the Reserve Officers Training Corps (ROTC), offered at many colleges and universities; Officer Candidate School (OCS) or Officer Training School (OTS); the National Guard (State Officer Candidate School programs); the Uniformed Services University of Health Sciences; and other programs. All are very selective and are good options for those wishing to make the military a career.

Federal service academies provide a four-year college program leading to a B.S. Midshipmen or cadets are provided free room and board, tuition, medical care, and a monthly allowance. Graduates receive regular or reserve commissions and have a five-year active duty obligation, or longer if entering flight training.

To become a candidate for appointment as a cadet or midshipman in one of the service academies, most applicants obtain a nomination from an authorized source (usually a member of Congress). Candidates do not need to know a member of Congress personally to request a nomination. Nominees must have an academic record of the requisite quality, college aptitude test scores above an established minimum, and recommendations from teachers or school officials; they must also pass a medical examination. Appointments are made from the list of eligible nominees. Appointments to the Coast Guard Academy, however, are made strictly on a competitive basis. A nomination is not required.

ROTC programs train students in about 950 army, 60 navy and Marine Corps, and 550 air force units at participating colleges and universities. Trainees take two to five hours of military instruction a week in addition to regular college courses. After graduation, they may serve as officers on active duty for a stipulated period of time. Some may serve their obligation in the reserves or National Guard. In the last two years of an ROTC program, students receive a monthly allowance while attending school and additional pay for summer training. ROTC scholarships for two, three, and four years are available on a competitive basis. All scholarships pay for tuition and have allowances for subsistence, textbooks, supplies, and other costs.

**Salaries**

The earnings structure for military personnel is shown in the following table. In 1999, most enlisted personnel started as recruits at Grade E-1. However, those with special skills or above-average education started as high as Grade E-4. Most warrant officers started at Grade W-1 or W-2, depending on their occupational and academic qualifications and the branch of service, but these individuals all had previous military service—this is not an entry-level occupation. Most commissioned officers started at Grade O-1, while some highly trained officers—for example, physicians, engineers, and scientists—started as high as Grade O-3 or O-4.

**Table 5.1   Military Basic Monthly Pay, January 1999**

| Grade | Less than 2 | 4+ | 8+ | 12+ | 16+ | 20+ |
|-------|-------------|-----|-----|------|------|------|
| | | | *Years of Service* | | | |
| O-9 | $6,947.10 | $7,281.00 | $7,466.10 | $7,776.90 | $8,425.80 | $8,892.60 |
| O-8 | $6,292.20 | $6,634.50 | $7,129.20 | $7,466.10 | $7,776.90 | $8,425.80 |
| O-7 | $5,228.40 | $5,583.90 | $5,834.40 | $6,172.50 | $7,129.20 | $7,619.70 |
| O-6 | $3,875.10 | $4,536.60 | $4,536.60 | $4,536.60 | $5,432.40 | $5,834.40 |
| O-5 | $3,099.60 | $3,891.00 | $3,891.00 | $4,224.30 | $4,845.00 | $5,277.90 |
| O-4 | $2,612.40 | $3,393.30 | $3,608.70 | $4,071.90 | $4,444.80 | $4,566.60 |
| O-3 | $2,427.60 | $3,210.60 | $3,484.80 | $3,855.30 | $3,949.50 | $3,949.50 |
| O-2 | $2,117.10 | $2,871.30 | $2,930.40 | $2,930.40 | $2,930.40 | $2,930.40 |
| O-1 | $1,838.10 | $2,312.10 | $2,312.10 | $2,312.10 | $2,312.10 | $2,312.10 |
| | | | | | | |
| W-5 | | | | | | $4,221.30 |
| W-4 | $2,473.20 | $2,714.10 | $2,962.80 | $3,303.00 | $3,578.00 | $3,792.00 |
| W-3 | $2,247.90 | $2,469.90 | $2,681.70 | $2,930.40 | $3,114.00 | $3,335.70 |
| W-2 | $1,968.90 | $2,192.10 | $2,438.40 | $2,623.80 | $2,809.50 | $2,993.10 |
| W-1 | $1,640.40 | $2,037.90 | $2,221.50 | $2,407.20 | $2,591.70 | $2,777.70 |

| Grade | Less than 2 | 4+ | 8+ | 12+ | 16+ | 20+ |
|-------|-------------|-----|-----|------|------|------|
| E-8 | | | $2,412.60 | $2,547.30 | $2,683.00 | $2,811.30 |
| E-7 | $1,684.80 | $1,952.10 | $2,082.90 | $2,216.70 | $2,383.00 | $2,480.40 |
| E-6 | $1,449.30 | $1,715.40 | $1,844.10 | $2,010.00 | $2,140.00 | $2,172.60 |
| E-5 | $1,271.70 | $1,514.70 | $1,680.30 | $1,811.10 | $1,844.10 | $1,844.10 |
| E-4 | $1,185.90 | $1,428.60 | $1,485.30 | $1,485.30 | $1,485.30 | $1,485.30 |
| E-3 | $1,179.80 | $1,274.70 | $1,274.70 | $1,274.70 | $1,274.70 | $1,274.70 |
| E-2 | $1,075.80 | $1,075.80 | $1,075.80 | $1,075.80 | $1,075.80 | $1,075.80 |
| E-1* | $959.40 | $959.40 | $959.40 | $959.40 | $959.40 | $959.40 |

*less than four months

Source: U.S. Department of Defense—Defense Finance and Accounting Service

## THE FOREIGN SERVICE

The Foreign Service falls under the jurisdiction of the State Department. In the field of foreign affairs, the State Department is placing increased emphasis on the language knowledge of its Foreign Service officers.

A career serving your country overseas can offer excitement, challenge, and even glamour. But being a part of the Foreign Service is more than just a job. It is a complete way of life that requires dedication and commitment.

**Positions Within the Foreign Service**

The Foreign Service divides the different specialty areas into the following "cones":

**Administration.** Administrative personnel at overseas posts are responsible for hiring foreign national workers, providing office and residential space, assuring reliable communications with Washington, D.C., supervising computer systems, and—of great importance in hostile or unfriendly areas—providing security for the post's personnel and property.

**Consular services.** Consular workers must often combine the skills of lawyers, judges, investigators, and social workers. Their duties range from issuing passports and visas to finding a lost child or helping a traveler in trouble.

**Economic officers.** Economic officers maintain contact with key business and financial leaders in the host country and report to Washington on the local economic conditions and their impact on American trade and investment policies. They are concerned with issues such as commercial aviation safety, fishing rights, and international banking.

**Political affairs.** Those working in political affairs analyze and report on the political views of the host country. They make contact with labor unions, humanitarian organizations, educators, and cultural leaders.

**Information and cultural affairs.** As part of the Foreign Service, the United States Information Agency (USIA) promotes U.S. cultural, informational, and public diplomacy programs. An information officer might develop a library open to the public, meet with the press, and oversee English language training programs for the host country.

**Commercial and business services.** In this division, Foreign Service officers identify overseas business connections for American exporters and investors, conduct market research for the success of U.S. products, and organize trade shows and other promotional events. They can be based in Washington, D.C., or can be sent anywhere in the world. They work at embassies, consulates, and other diplomatic missions in major cities or small towns. They help the thousands of Americans traveling and living overseas, issue visas to citizens of other countries wishing to visit the United States, and help our government execute our foreign policies.

Foreign Service workers can experience a glamorous lifestyle, dining with their ambassador in a European palace, meeting royalty or other heads of state. They can be present at important decision-making sessions and influence world politics and history. But postings can offer hardship as well, in environments as hostile as Antarctica or a Middle East desert. Some postings are in isolated locations without the familiar comforts of home. The weather can be harsh, and there can be health hazards. Danger from unrest or war is always possible.

In spite of the difficulties, those in the Foreign Service are happy with its unique rewards and opportunities.

## Training

Although many Foreign Service officers are skilled in political science and history, these days candidates can have knowledge in specialized fields such as the environment, computer science, the fight against AIDS, antidrug efforts, and trade.

There are several steps to complete to apply for a position in the Foreign Service:

**Written examination.** This is a daylong multiple-choice test usually given once a year. It measures verbal and numerical reasoning, political and cultural awareness, English language expression, and knowledge of topics important to the function of the Foreign Service. It's a difficult exam, and many people have to take it more than once before they pass.

**Oral evaluation.** Those who pass the written exam are invited to participate in an all-day oral assessment. It tests the skills, abilities, knowledge, and personal characteristics necessary to succeed in the Foreign Service. Writing skills are measured, as well as administrative, problem-solving, leadership, and interpersonal skills.

**Medical clearance.** Because many postings have inadequate health care or pose health hazards, candidates for the Foreign Service must meet a high medical standard. Allowances are made, however, for certain disabilities.

**Background investigation.** The Department of State, along with other federal, state, and local agencies, conducts a thorough background check on Foreign Service candidates. They examine employment records, credit history, repayment of school loans, drug abuse, and criminal records.

**Eligibility**

Before you can take the Foreign Service written examination you must be:

- at least twenty years old on the date of the exam

- no more than fifty-nine years old

- a citizen of the United States

- available for worldwide assignment

**Job Outlook**

The Foreign Service exam is not offered on a yearly basis. Rather, it is given when there are definite positions to fill. Because competition is keen for all positions, the number of candidates nearly always exceeds the number of openings. Most openings arise from the need to replace Foreign Service workers who retire or leave the profession for other reasons.

**Salaries**

The starting salary is generally low, but it may be increased at overseas posts with free housing, furniture, utilities, travel expenses, educational allowances for children, and cost of living allowances in high-cost cities. Extra pay is also given for dangerous and "hardship" posts.

## DEPARTMENT OF DEFENSE DEPENDENTS SCHOOLS

The Department of Defense operates schools, K through 12, in overseas areas to provide American-style public school education for minor dependents of active duty military and civilian personnel.

Qualifications for a teaching position within DoDDS include U.S. citizenship, a bachelor's degree from an accredited institution, eighteen semester hours in education courses, student teaching or an internship, and good physical condition. At least one full year of professional teaching experience within the past five years in the grade or subject for which one is applying is preferable. Usually secondary teachers must fully qualify by education and/or experience in two subject fields (e.g., a foreign language and physical education; social studies and art).

**To Apply**

The processing of requests for employment is conducted by the Department of Defense Education Activity. Applications for teaching positions are accepted year-round. Teachers are encouraged to apply by January for employment during the following school year. Department of Defense contact information is provided at the end of this chapter.

## U.S. CUSTOMS

The U.S. Customs Service is a federal law enforcement agency that has protected our borders—land, sea, and air—for more than two hundred years. Today, one of its primary duties is to keep illegal drugs out of the country. Other U.S. Customs missions include a wide range of import/export inspections, collection of duties, and inspection of personal goods being brought into the country. Customs also works closely with other federal agencies to ensure the overall security of U.S. borders.

U.S. Customs hires a variety of personnel, including customs inspectors, canine enforcement officers, criminal investigators (special agents), import specialists, and pilots.

**Requirements and Qualifications**

Four years of college or three years of work experience will usually meet the requirement for an entry-level (GS-5) position. A combination of college and work experience is acceptable. To qualify for a GS-7 grade level, you must have at least one year of specialized experience in import/export or compliance/regulatory work. Collegiate academic excellence or graduate education can also help fulfill requirements for a GS-7. Prior law enforcement or military service is often a good starting point for a Customs career. Although not stated as a requirement, knowledge of a foreign language such as Spanish would certainly give applicants an edge.

You also need to be a U.S. citizen with a valid driver's license and must successfully complete a thorough background investigation and medical and drug screenings.

Eleven weeks of rigorous physical and educational training at the Federal Law Enforcement Training Center is required of every recruit. Firearms training is also required, and inspectors must continue to maintain firearms proficiency.

Inspectors frequently have responsibility for valuable goods, seized drugs, and currency, so absolute integrity is essential. An inspector must be a people person and have a mature emotional balance in order to stay cool and make rapid decisions in volatile situations.

A Customs career demands both physical stamina and mental discipline. Nearly all assignments require being on your feet for long hours, and many duties, particularly at land borders, are physically demanding. (See the following section, Department of Justice: Border Patrol Agents.)

In some assignments, inspectors have to climb aboard train cars, trucks, and into ships' holds. Inspectors at land borders and in harbors work outdoors in all kinds of weather. Some tasks involve getting dirty going through cargo and tearing apart vehicles in search of drugs. And, although duties are nearly always performed in a controlled environment, officers carry firearms and are sometimes called upon to use them. The wide variety of ports in which the United States operates means not only that there is a great diversity of duties but also that some assignments entail significantly greater law enforcement challenges than others.

## DEPARTMENT OF JUSTICE: BORDER PATROL AGENTS

Candidates for Border Patrol agent positions with the Immigration and Naturalization Service (INS) must pass a drug test, a background investigation, and a stringent preemployment medical examination.

You must be physically able to perform strenuous duties under rigorous environmental conditions. Duties require physical stamina in running long distances, climbing, jumping, withstanding exposure to extreme weather conditions for extended periods, and standing and stooping for long periods. Irregular and protracted work hours are also common. Binocular vision is required, and uncorrected vision must test at least 20/100 in each eye. Any disease or condition that interferes with the safe, efficient, and expected performance of the job duties or required training may constitute grounds for medical disqualification.

Public Law 100-38 established a maximum entry age for Border Patrol agent positions. You must be less than thirty-seven years old at the time you are first hired.

Border Patrol agents must be able to speak and read Spanish well. All applicants must pass a written test to demonstrate their ability to speak, or to learn, Spanish. In addition, all applicants must be willing to learn Spanish during training at the Border Patrol Academy.

## CENTRAL INTELLIGENCE AGENCY (CIA)

*Innovative* and *intriguing* are two words the CIA uses to describe itself. The CIA supports the president, the National Security Council, and all who make and execute U.S. national security policy by providing accurate, evidence-based, comprehensive, and timely foreign intelligence related to national security. This agency also conducts counterintelligence activities, special activities, and other functions related to foreign intelligence and national security as directed by the president.

**Training to Work for the CIA**

All new CIA employees attend a basic orientation, and most receive on-the-job and formal classroom training through a wide variety of internal courses. Employees may also be sponsored for external university and professional training, both full time and part time, in programs relevant to their jobs. Some of the universities in the Washington, D.C., area are the University of Virginia,

University of Maryland, Georgetown, George Washington, Johns Hopkins, Howard, Gallaudet, George Mason, Virginia Tech, and Marymount.

The Agency has a complete library with an excellent reference service and an extensive collection of national and international newspapers and periodicals. There is a self-study center and a language school. Cash awards are available for attaining and maintaining competence in certain foreign languages. With that in mind, the CIA has ongoing needs for language instructors on a permanent or temporary basis.

The CIA seeks professionals with native fluency in Arabic, Chinese, Croatian, Farsi, French, German, Indonesian, Italian, Greek, Japanese, Korean, Serbian, Thai, and Vietnamese, and with expertise in sign language. Qualifications include a degree in language, linguistics, education, or a related field, and a background and/or interest in working with adult learners. Salary is $125 to $175 per day for temporary instructors, depending on experience and credentials. Applicants must successfully complete a background investigation and a polygraph examination. U.S. citizenship is required.

Here are two sample job announcements issued by the CIA:

## FRENCH LANGUAGE INSTRUCTOR

The CIA is looking for a part-time contract Language Instructor to provide foreign language instruction within the Agency's Office of Training and Education. Instructors are responsible for teaching reading, speaking, and understanding to all levels and types of students. In addition, instructors develop training materials for classroom use, plan courses, participate in total immersion exercises, and arrange for travel with students to areas where the language being learned is in use. Classes run from three to eighteen months in length.

Applicants are being sought at the Developmental Level, which pays from a GS-9 ($35,310) to GS-12 ($66,564) range. Naturally, starting pay is adjusted to reflect prior experience and language abilities.

Qualifications: Must have a minimum of a bachelor's degree (or equivalent) in language, linguistics, education, or related field, and educated native fluency in French. Candidates also must have excellent interpersonal and communications skills, as well as knowledge of the principles of adult learning and of curriculum design and development. All applicants must be U.S. citizens and be able to earn/maintain a security clearance via a National Security Background Investigation.

## INTERPRETERS—SIGN LANGUAGE

The Central Intelligence Agency is looking for qualified sign language interpreters to work in the Washington, D.C., metropolitan area. The individuals selected will serve on a contractual basis. Applicants must have at least three years professional interpreting experience. Certification is preferred but not required. Applicants must successfully complete an interpreter evaluation panel review, a polygraph interview, and an extensive background investigation. U.S. citizenship is required. Salary is dependent upon qualifications.

To apply, submit your résumé on-line at www.odci.gov/ or mail your résumé and cover letter to:

Recruitment Center
Attn: Language Instructor
P.O. Box 4090, Department INTERNET
Reston, VA 20195

## PEACE CORPS

This program's slogan is "Peace Corps: The Toughest Job You'll Ever Love." For four decades the Peace Corps has worked to foster international peace and friendship, encourage grassroots development in the world's poorest nations, and build greater understanding of the world among Americans. More than 148,000 Americans have served as Peace Corps volunteers since the agency was founded in 1961. Today, nearly 6,500 serve in ninety countries around the world, providing assistance in education, health, agriculture, environmental issues, and business development.

**Opportunities**

The Peace Corps offers trained men and women a chance to gain important international experience, challenge themselves personally, and help solve the world's pressing problems. Employers in government and the private sector value the experience acquired by Peace Corps volunteers.

Peace Corps assignments emphasize appropriate technology and cultural sensitivity. Serving two years, volunteers work in a variety of fields, usually at the community level:

| | |
|---|---|
| Agriculture | Forestry and Environment |
| Economic Development | Health and Nutrition Education |
| Engineering | Industrial Arts |

**Qualifications**

Most assignments require a bachelor's degree, but some may require an additional three to five years of work experience; others may require a master's degree. Graduates in liberal arts fields must have demonstrated skills requested by Peace Corps host countries. Selection from among liberal arts candidates is highly competitive. You must be a U.S. citizen and at least 18 years old. There is no upper age limit. Married couples are welcome but difficult to place. The Peace Corps does not place families with dependent children.

**Training**

New volunteers receive eight to twelve weeks of intensive language, cultural, and technical training. Periodic in-service workshops assist volunteers in planning projects, reinforcing skills, and learning new skills.

**Benefits**

During service, volunteers receive a monthly allowance for food, clothing, and incidentals. They also receive free medical and dental care, vacation time, and transportation to and from their overseas sites. Most student loan payments are deferred for the duration of Peace Corps service, and a partial loan cancellation program is available.

**What the Work Is Like**

Peace Corps volunteers live in both rural and urban settings at the level of their host country counterparts. They work with host country agencies or institutions and also maintain contact with Peace Corps staff. Often, volunteers share work sites with, or are located near, other volunteers. Although they leave family and friends behind in the United States, many volunteers feel that one of the most rewarding aspects of the experience is making new friends and being welcomed into the host country culture.

Following Peace Corps service, volunteers receive a readjustment allowance of approximately $5,400. They receive job hunting assistance from the Peace Corps and are eligible for federal employment on a noncompetitive basis. More than fifty institutions offer special scholarships and assistantships for returning volunteers. The Peace Corps Fellows/USA program can open doors for returned volunteers by providing part-time employment in underserved communities while they attend graduate school. There is even a way to get academic credit for certain Peace Corps training.

**To Apply**

If you are interested in becoming a Peace Corps volunteer, call 800-424-8580 and choose option one. This will put you in touch with your local recruiter, who will discuss your options and send you an application and any additional information you request. The application process can take up to one year, so plan accordingly.

If you are interested in an administrative position at Peace Corps headquarters, call 800-818-9579 for current job listings. Or visit www.peacecorps.gov.

## AMERICORPS—THE NATIONAL SERVICE PLAN

AmeriCorps is the new national service movement that engages thousands of Americans of all ages and backgrounds in a domestic Peace Corps to get things done throughout our nation's urban and rural communities. In the spirit of the Peace Corps, AmeriCorps offers life-changing experiences that extend to lifetime legacies of service and citizenship.

In exchange for one to two years of results-driven service, Americans receive a living allowance averaging $7,500 per year, health care, child care when needed, and an education award of $4,725 per year to finance higher education or to pay back student loans. Under certain circumstances, you could serve part time and receive an education award of $2,362 per year.

AmeriCorps offers a variety of time options for service. You can serve after high school or during or after college, graduate school, or vocational training. And you can serve at home right in your own community or in any other part of the country.

**To Apply**

Contact the AmeriCorps hot line at 800-942-2677 to request a National Referral Form. When you complete the form and return it, you automatically become part of the AmeriCorps National Service Network Database that is used to supply local AmeriCorps members with national recruits. You will also receive a list of AmeriCorps programs so that you can contact them directly to request their local application forms. Visit www.americorps.org for more information.

## HISPANIC EMPLOYMENT INITIATIVE

The U.S. Office of Personnel Management has launched a Hispanic Employment Initiative by which federal agencies can improve the representation of Hispanics in the federal workforce.

**Nine-Point Plan**

The Nine-Point Plan is the initiative's strategy to recruit, advance, and retain qualified Hispanic candidates in the federal workforce.

1. Support and implement the White House Initiative on Educational Excellence for Hispanic Americans by matching job opportunities with curriculums of Hispanic Serving Institutions.

2. Provide employment information to students, faculty, and members of the Hispanic community.

3. Use the Presidential Management Intern Program (PMIP) for recruiting, converting, and advancing Hispanic college graduates.

4. Participate in the Hispanic Association of Colleges and Universities (HACU) internship program.

5. Use the Student Educational Employment Program as a tool to recruit Hispanic students.

6. Develop mentoring programs to motivate young Hispanic people to pursue a federal civil service career.

7. Promote participation of Hispanic employees in career development programs.

8. Assess the need for Hispanic Employment Program (HEP) managers in federal agencies.

9. Monitor the progress of recruiting and training Hispanic employees.

**Resources**

Here are some of the resources available to assist Hispanic Americans in starting a search for a career in the federal civil service.

**Bilingual/bicultural program.** Bilingual/bicultural authority provides employment opportunities at the entry level for professional and administrative positions that call for Spanish language skills or knowledge of Hispanic culture to enhance job performance.

**Student volunteer service.** High school and college student volunteers engage in professional projects and work activities related to their academic studies. Activities range from developing computer skills to researching projects involving wildlife initiatives, environmental concerns, and congressional issues.

**Student Educational Employment Program.** This program gives you a jump start in your chosen career by providing valuable, paid-work experience while you are still in school. Opportunities can range from summer jobs to positions that last for as long as you are enrolled in school. See the next section for information on specific opportunities.

**Outstanding Scholar Program.** College graduates with a GPA of at least 3.5 or who have graduated in the upper 10 percent of their class can apply for positions under the Outstanding Scholar hiring authority, which offers many entry-level positions in diverse fields.

**HACU internship program.** The HACU internship program provides employment opportunities for students who are interested in gaining job experience in diverse fields across the government. There are ten-week internships during the spring, summer, and fall semesters. However, HACU interns are not federal employees. For more information, call HACU at 202-467-0893.

**Federal jobs.** The federal civil service has more than twelve thousand job vacancies worldwide every day. You can find information and apply by accessing the federal government's official job information system, USAJOBS, at www.usajobs.opm.gov.

## STUDENT EDUCATIONAL EMPLOYMENT PROGRAM

Through this program you can gain valuable work experience while you're still in school . . . and get paid for it!

The U.S. Office of Personnel Management (OPM) has consolidated its Cooperative Education, Stay-in-School, Federal Junior Fellowship, and Summer Aid programs into the new Student Educational Employment Program. It combines key features of the old programs with added flexibilities to produce a more effective and streamlined program.

The federal government has always looked to educational institutions to find people who have the skills needed to meet its future employment needs. Most federal agencies use this program. Some develop additional student, intern, or fellowship programs to meet their specific business needs. No matter what agency you choose, the Student Educational Employment Program will introduce you to the advantages and challenges of working for the U.S. government.

**The Components**

The program has two components: student temporary employment and student career experience. It is available to all levels of students: high school, vocational and technical, associate degree, baccalaureate degree, graduate degree, and professional degree. Temporary employment can range from summer jobs to positions that can last for as long as you are a student. These employment opportunities need not necessarily be related to your academic field of study. The career experience component offers you valuable work experience directly related to your field of study. It provides formal periods of work and study while you are attending school. It requires a commitment by you, your school, and the employing federal agency. You may be eligible for permanent employment after successfully completing your education and meeting work requirements.

Students may contact their school guidance office, career planning and placement office, teachers, or the federal agency employment office where they are interested in working. They may also visit the OPM website at www.opm.gov/employ/students/index.htm.

## STUDENT INTERNSHIP PROGRAMS WITH THE FEDERAL GOVERNMENT

Some federal agencies have developed agency-specific programs, but this internship listing is limited to special programs that can be used for hiring in all federal agencies. Some interns are paid according to the civil service general schedule; refer to the schedule on page 53 as needed.

**Hispanic Association of Colleges and Universities' National Internship Program (HNIP)**

Sponsoring organization: Hispanic Association of Colleges and Universities (HACU)

National Headquarters
8415 Datapoint Drive, Suite 400
San Antonio, TX 78229
210-692-3805
www.hacu.com

Washington, D.C., Office
One Dupont Circle NW, Suite 605
Washington, DC 20036
202-467-0893

HNIP interns are employees of HACU. The interns are placed in federal agencies that participate through a contractual or cooperative agreement with HACU. Although HNIP interns are employees of HACU, they must comply with the work schedule of the participating federal department/agency and submit time sheets that indicate the number of hours worked. Only after submitting a time sheet with the signature of their immediate supervisor will interns receive a stipend. Interns are not paid overtime, do not accrue vacation, and are not eligible for unemployment benefits. Internships are for ten weeks, beginning in June and ending in August. Internships are also available during the fall and spring semesters. HNIP places interns nationwide, in the Washington, D.C., metropolitan area, and Puerto Rico.

**Congressional Hispanic Caucus Institute's Fellowship Program (CHCI)**

Sponsoring organization: Congressional Hispanic Caucus Institute, Inc. (CHCI)

504 C Street NE
Washington, DC 20002
www.chci.org

The program is conducted nine months out of the year for thirty-six weeks from early September to late May. CHCI places interns in the Washington, D.C., metropolitan area only.

**Presidential Management Intern Program (PMIP)**

Sponsoring organization: U.S. Office of Personnel Management

OPM Service Center
William Green Federal Building
600 Arch Street
Philadelphia, PA 19106-1596
www.pmi.opm.gov. Complete details are on the website.

**Minority Leaders Fellowship Program (MLFP)**

Sponsoring organization: The Washington Center for Internships and Academic Affairs

1101 Fourteenth Street NW, Suite 500
Washington, DC 20005-5622
www.twc.edu

Fellowships are available in the fall and spring semesters for fourteen to fifteen weeks, while summer internships are ten weeks in duration. MLFP internships are available in the Washington, D.C., metropolitan area.

**Workforce Recruitment Program for College Students with Disabilities (WRP)**

Sponsoring organizations: The President's Committee on Employment of People with Disabilities and the U.S. Department of Defense

The President's Committee on Employment
    of People with Disabilities
1131 F Street NW, Third Floor
Washington, DC 20004-1107

Interns are paid according to their level of education and enter the civil service between the GS-2 and GS-9 grade levels. Departments/agencies may offer participants permanent positions if they are graduating seniors or graduate students.

**White House Fellows Program**

Sponsoring organization: President's Commission on White House Fellowships

712 Jackson Place NW
Washington, DC 20503
www.whitehousefellows.gov/home.html

Fellows receive a salary and benefit package from the department/agency to which they are assigned. Compensation is commensurate with the federal pay grade GS-14, step 3. These one-year fellowships begin on September 1 and end on August 31. White House Fellowships are all in Washington, D.C.

**Asian Pacific American Institute for Congressional Studies' Summer Internship Program**

Sponsoring organization: Asian Pacific American Institute for Congressional Studies

209 Pennsylvania Avenue SE, Suite 100
Washington, DC 20003
www.capaci.org.

Interns receive a $2,500 stipend from the Institute and are expected to make their own travel and housing arrangements. Internships are from early June through early August each year. These internships are all in the Washington, D.C., metropolitan area.

**Organization of Chinese Americans' Congressional and Government Internships**

Sponsoring organization: Organization of Chinese Americans, Inc. (OCA)

1001 Connecticut Avenue NW, Suite 707
Washington, DC 20036
www.ocanatl.org

Interns receive a $1,500 stipend from OCA for ten weeks of full-time work. Interns are responsible for transportation to and from Washington, D.C., and housing. Internships are available in the spring, summer, and fall in Washington, D.C., only.

**Washington Internships for Native American Students (WINS)**

Sponsoring organization: American University/Washington Internships for Native American Students

4400 Massachusetts Avenue NW
Washington, DC 20016
www.american.edu/other.depts/wins

Agencies are paid $6,300 per intern (in 1998) to participate in the WINS program. That covers the intern's tuition, round-trip travel to Washington, D.C., local transportation, housing, a meal plan, costs associated with social and cultural activities, and a stipend of $150 per week. Interns, however, are responsible for incidental expenses for nonprogram activities, such as medical care and independent social activities. Students receive six credit hours for participating in this program. WINS internships are all in the Washington, D.C., metropolitan area.

**INROADS/Greater Washington Internships**

Sponsoring organization: INROADS

INROADS/Greater Washington, Inc.
1010 Wayne Avenue, Suite 555
Silver Spring, MD 20910-5600

INROADS, Inc., National Headquarters
St. Louis, MO 63102
www.inroadsinc.org

Participating agencies pay the cost for interns selected through the INROADS Internship organization ($3,000 plus the wages earned by interns). INROADS prefers to finalize all internship placements between early March and the end of April. Summer internships are typically for ten weeks, and they begin and end according to the intern's educational schedule. While INROADS/Greater Washington, Inc., places interns only in the Washington, D.C., metropolitan area, internships are available in over fifty affiliate offices around the country.

Since the interns hired in the respective metropolitan areas usually live and attend school in the area, housing and transportation during the internship session are unnecessary. Wages are commensurate with the intern's educational level and typically range between the GS-3 and GS-7 grade levels.

**NAFEO Services, Inc. Summer Intern Program**

Sponsoring organization: NAFEO Services, Inc.

Intern Programs
5214 Baltimore Avenue, Suite 200
Hyattsville, MD 20781

The cost to participating departments and agencies for NAFEO Services interns was about $8,350 per intern in 1998, regardless of whether the intern was an undergraduate or graduate student. The cost covers round-trip travel expenses to Washington, D.C., or to the intern's work site plus a stipend commensurate with the intern's educational level and training. In addition, NAFEO Services assists interns in locating housing. Most students are responsible for housing costs. Summer internships are for ten weeks, beginning in June and ending in August. NAFEO Services also administers internships in the fall and spring. NAFEO Services places interns nationwide and in the Washington, D.C., metropolitan area.

**AISES Student Summer Work Experience Program**

Sponsoring organization: American Indian Science and Engineering Society (AISES)

5661 Airport Boulevard
Boulder, CO 80301-2339
www.aises.org

The stipend is approximately $8,575, which includes salaries, benefits, and round-trip travel expenses. AISES arranges the housing for interns working in Washington, D.C., but interns are responsible for their lodging costs. AISES helps American Indian students prepare for careers in science, technology, engineering, business, and other academic areas. The Summer Work Experience Program begins in early June and extends for a ten-week period into mid-August. AISES places interns in Washington, D.C., and nationwide.

**Women in Public Policy Internship Program (WIPP)**

Sponsoring organization: The Washington Center for Internships and Academic Affairs

1101 Fourteenth Street NW, Suite 500
Washington, DC 20005-5622
www.twc.edu

Interns are responsible for round-trip transportation to Washington, D.C., local transportation, meals, and a program fee. The program fee for the 1997 summer term was $2,450, and for the fall term, $2,750. While the Washington Center offers financial assistance, approximately 35 percent of students receive no financial assistance, and awards are generally limited to $2,000. To be considered for financial assistance, students must live in Washington Center housing. Scholarship awards are first applied to the housing fee, which was $1,825 for the summer term and $2,575 for the fall term. However, you should call the Washington Center for current program and housing fees. Internships in the Washington, D.C., metropolitan area are available during the summer, fall, and spring semesters.

In addition to using the above contact information, students may contact their school guidance office, career planning and placement office, teachers, or the federal agency employment office where they are interested in working. They may also visit the OPM website at www.opm.gov/employ/students/index.htm.

## FIRSTHAND ACCOUNTS

### Jim Van Laningham
### Foreign Service Officer

Jim Van Laningham has made the Foreign Service his career for more than twenty years. He's been posted in Russia in the former Soviet Union, Poland, Morocco, Iraq, Thailand, and Washington, D.C. He is a general service officer, which falls under the administration cone.

**Getting Started**

"I became interested about the time I was in junior high school. I had just read the book, *The Ugly American*, and it talked about the image of Americans overseas and how Foreign Service officers helped correct what often was a bad image. It got me thinking about it.

"I earned a bachelor's degree in economics then went on for a master's in international business. I took the Foreign Service exam right after I graduated so all the information was still fresh. My education was very helpful.

"It was a year and a half from the time I took the exam until I was accepted. I was very excited. They called me up one day and asked if I could be there in less than a month. They wanted an answer right away. My wife and I discussed it and decided to take the plunge. We went to Washington, and they gave me about two months of training in a basic orientation course for new officers and six months of language training. After that I was assigned to the embassy in Moscow as an economics officer. But today it's almost mandatory that the first tour for most Foreign Service officers is as a consular officer, issuing visas to people who want to come to the United States."

**What the Work Is Like**     "An administrative officer is the person responsible for keeping the embassy operating on a day-to-day basis. First thing in the morning I might find a series of cables from Washington waiting for me, which would require me to report on certain information. Depending on the time of the year, I may be involved in renewing leases on houses we rent for our American staff, or I may be involved in preparing the budget for the embassy, which could be anywhere from a million dollars and up. The budget covers salaries of embassy staff; electricity and other utilities; and procurement of paper, pencils, computers, copy machines, and other office equipment. For lunch I may meet with several of my counterparts from other embassies, administrative officers from Australia or Canada or Great Britain, to discuss issues. Later on in the day, I may be involved in personnel issues in which I evaluate employee performance and recommend promotion. Or I may have a discipline problem with an employee and have to talk to him about it. I'm even responsible for firing someone if necessary.

"Entertaining is a big part of a Foreign Service officer's life—having local people or people from other embassies to dinner, or going to dinner at someone else's house. Oftentimes you learn a lot about what's going on in the country from talking to other diplomats or the people who live there.

"On weekends you can travel around the country, go to other cities and see what there is to see. Not only to play tourist but also to meet other people and talk to them."

**The Upsides and Downsides**     "What I like most about being an administrative officer in the Foreign Service is the opportunity to see a problem, determine the solution, and then see it through to the end. Obviously, travel is also a very attractive part of the job. You can live overseas in a country for a number of years and really get to know in depth what it's like. And for me there's a lot of excitement about being able to represent the United States overseas, meeting important people in the country where you are living and perhaps even affecting how relations develop between the United States and that country.

"I was posted in Iraq at the time Saddam Hussein invaded Kuwait. I had been scheduled to fly home to attend my high school reunion, but of course there were no planes leaving the country, and I couldn't get out. We were able to evacuate most of the staff of the American embassy in Baghdad, and then we had about one hundred people from the embassy in Kuwait who were trying to get back to the United States. Although, originally, we were given permission for them to leave, it turned out they were not able to. A lot of my time for about three days was spent trying to get exit visas. The permission finally came through at about three o'clock in the morning, Iraqi time.

"I suddenly remembered that that was the exact time my high school reunion had been scheduled. I knew the telephone number where the reunion was being held, so I called and ended up talking to about forty of my former classmates over the phone. That and having just succeeded in getting visas for a hundred people to get out of the country made for a wonderful experience, one that I won't quickly forget.

"Another benefit of working with the Foreign Service is that you can retire at age fifty with twenty years of service.

"There are always some downsides, however. When you have a very large organization like the State Department and a lot of different officers with various interests, and you're working on a problem for which it's necessary to get the approval of all those officers on any action you want to take, it can be time consuming and frustrating. And as the U.S. government and the State Department face shrinking budgets, there's less money to accomplish things.

"As frustrating as it can be at times, it's a fabulous career. There's no such thing as a regular routine, and every day you can have a new challenge in front of you. For me it's a fun way of life."

**Advice from Jim Van Laningham**

"You have to be able to write well, to organize thoughts logically and coherently. You have to be outgoing because you deal with a lot of different people, and you have to have people skills. I think you have to be interested in the world and what's going on around you because a lot of what you do is report back to Washington on what's happening in the country you're in. And if you're in the administration cone, hopefully you are a good manager of people. You have to have leadership ability. It also helps to be familiar with finances and budgets.

"I don't think any one particular field of study leads to the Foreign Service. The people I've met have taken every imaginable major in school. It's more just studying well and doing well and getting a well-rounded education."

## Arthur Fern
## Government and Independent Consultant

Arthur Fern is retired now, but he worked for many years in international relations in a variety of capacities, including the following:

U.S. Army, Counterintelligence Corps agent in West Berlin
U.S. Treasury, Office of International Finance, Financial Economist
Joint Economic Committee of Congress, consultant to the Subcommittee on Foreign Trade
U.S. Embassy, Bonn, West Germany, Assistant Financial Attaché
Independent consultant, contracts with the Japanese embassy, the U.S. Treasury, and German and Swiss firms interested in World Bank business.
Founder/owner/manager of a consulting/representation firm (foreign trade and finance), concentrating on projects of the multilateral financial institutions (World Bank Group and Inter-American Development Bank) in Washington with German, Swiss, French, and Dutch clients.

Arthur Fern earned his B.A. in economics from Washington and Lee University in Lexington, Virginia, in 1955. He earned his M.A. in international relations in 1961 from the School of Advanced International Studies of Johns Hopkins University, Washington, D.C. He also participated in various nondegree courses in business, foreign languages, and writing.

**Getting Started**

"Although I'm retired now, I spoke fluent German when I was with counterintelligence in Berlin and at the U.S. Embassy in Bonn, passable French when I worked with a French consulting firm on World Bank projects, and had walk-around Spanish when working on projects in South America. I've been to some forty countries—mostly on business but also touring. I worked with German, French, and Dutch companies on World Bank projects.

"My first interest stemmed from letters from my uncle, a U.S. Army ranger. He served in North Africa, was in the fourth wave on Omaha Beach on D day, in the Battle of the Bulge and Huertgen Forest, and a German POW. When I was fourteen, I got my amateur radio license and started communicating with countries overseas in CW (Morse code)—Johannesburg, Tokyo, Moscow, London, and the like. It was fun. The grades I received in French in high school and college were some of my best. I truly think my Latin and a year of ancient Greek helped. It all converged in college—I aimed at courses and interests that were international.

"The draft was still in force when I graduated from college. The Korean War was in a stalemate. I reasoned it would be better to enlist for three years and pick my duty and training than to be drafted and serve for two years as a clerk. So I selected the army's Counterintelligence Corps. Following agent training at Fort Holabird, I was sent to German language school in Stuttgart and took a German course at the Technische Hochschule evenings and weekends. After that I was assigned to Berlin.

"I read the *Berliner Morgenpost* every morning, building up my vocabulary. I dated German women and attended German, not PX, movies. Except for writing reports in the office, we were indeed living on the local economy, as the expression goes. You can really say you're getting a grip on a foreign language when you start to dream in it—and l did."

**What the Work Was Like**

"Although it was a good, very good, two and a half years in Berlin—and I could have stayed—I decided to go to graduate school for international relations with a major in economics. Next stop: the Office of International Finance at the U.S. Treasury for a couple of years (my office overlooked the helicopter pad of the White House). Although this span was mostly in English, I did assist the undersecretary in a few courtesy meetings with French-speaking ministers from Africa during the IMF/World Bank meetings in Washington.

"In 1963, the Treasury assigned me as Assistant Financial Attaché to the U.S. Embassy in Bonn. Duties were principally reporting on German monetary and fiscal matters, i.e., liaison with the Ministry of Finance and the Bundesbank in Frankfurt, reviewing the economic and financial news. An oddity of embassy social life was the unwritten rule that each member of a large gathering could speak his or her own language and the others would understand. Many of the spouses didn't speak a foreign language. It did seem a bit strange to hear the wife of a Spanish diplomat ask a question in Spanish, the German official answer in German, and the Frenchman add his two cents in French. A Canadian might come back in English, French, or German. Canadian foreign service personnel are required to have both English and French. Truly an international party!

"Subsequent to my stint with the embassy I left the government, having decided to go independent. One of my first assignments as a consultant was to do a study of private foreign investment in Latin America for the Japanese embassy in Washington.

"U.S. statistics on the subject were the most complete, but of course we used Spanish and other sources, too. I visited the Japanese financial attaché to deliver an interim report, and he handed me the Portuguese version of the *Economist* of London. He said I should definitely use this latest information. I apologized that I didn't speak any Portuguese, that I was restricted to English, German, French, and Spanish. 'But, Mr. Fern,' he replied, 'they are all Western languages from a common root system. We didn't expect you to have any Eastern languages.'

"My consulting business evolved more and more in the direction of the World Bank. I visited the German-American Chamber of Commerce in New York to drum up business. By the luck of the draw—my German and background in international economics prepared me for the opportunity—I had a contract the next morning. The standard operating procedure of the German and Swiss companies was that they would correspond in German, and I in English. Personal visits in Washington and Europe were in German.

"For the most part, credit negotiations at the World Bank Group are in the official language of the borrowing country. For example, even though the negotiating ministers spoke their local tribal languages, the loan negotiations were in French with the documents in both English and French."

**Upsides and Downsides** "I loved the fascinating personalities and quirky situations, and that boredom was at an absolute minimum. And, at times, I thought I was contributing to the world in some small way.

"What I liked the least was that as a consultant I often worked on a retainer plus bonus or commission basis. There was some stability to income [in that he knew he would meet a minimum], but there were also wide swings in income."

**Salaries** "In the army, I think I earned about $300 or so a month plus allowances for food and civilian clothes, and I lived in a 'safe house' on the local economy. I started with the Treasury after graduate school for $5,900 per year. My income as an independent consultant varied—sometimes it was bad and other times it was quite handsome. My travel was either reimbursed or at least deductible as a business expense."

**Advice from Arthur Fern**    "I know this will sound corny, but the old adage 'know thyself' still holds true. I loved international relations, but back in the fifties, sixties, and seventies it was dominated by big organizations—the big banks, the oil companies, the Big Three in Detroit, and, of course, big government. My father was a sole practitioner as a doctor, and many of our friends were small businessmen. I didn't realize until I was in my thirties how this latent urge to be my own boss would emerge or how strongly. The question became how to marry the urge to be a small business in an arena overshadowed by huge organizations.

"By preparing yourself (and foreign languages are a strong factor), you're at least laying the platform for opportunity and luck to find you.

"Regarding specific advice on foreign languages, always keep a pocket dictionary and small notebook with you. If you see an advertising sign on a bus in Tegucigalpa and don't understand it, jot it down and go over it before bed and the next morning, too. But remember, no matter how many foreign languages you acquire, or how well you acquire them, they are ancillary to your functional, substantive field, be it engineering, medicine, finance, or whatever."

## FOR MORE INFORMATION

### Teaching
Department of Defense Education Activity
Attn: Teacher Recruitment
4040 North Fairfax Drive
Arlington, VA 22203-1634
703-696-3068

### Interpreting
U.S. Department of State
Language Services Division, Room 2212
2201 C Street NW
Washington, DC 20520
202-647-3492

### Translating
U.S. Department of State
Language Services Division, Room 2204
2201 C Street NW
Washington, DC 20520
202-647-2201

### Customs Inspectors
Visit their website at www.customs.ustreas.gov or call 800-944-7725 for career information.

U.S. Customs Service
1301 Constitution Avenue NW
Washington, DC 20415

**Military**
Each of the military services publishes handbooks, fact sheets, and pamphlets describing entrance requirements, training and advancement opportunities, and other aspects of military careers. These publications are widely available at all recruiting stations; most state employment service offices; and in high schools, colleges, and public libraries. Information on educational and other veterans' benefits is available from VA offices throughout the country.

Excepted Service Agencies
Federal Reserve System Board of Governors
20th and C Street NW
Washington, DC 20551

Central Intelligence Agency
Office of Personnel
Washington, DC 20505

Defense Intelligence Agency
Civilian Personnel Office DAH-2
100 MacDill Boulevard
Washington, DC 20340-5100

U.S. Department of State
Foreign Service Positions, Recruitment Division
P.O. Box 9317, Rosslyn Station
Arlington, VA 22219

Federal Bureau of Investigation
JEH Building, Room 6647
10th Street and Pennsylvania Avenue NW
Washington, DC 20571

General Accounting Office
441 G Street NW, Room 1157
Washington, DC 20548

International Agency for Development (AID)
2401 E Street NW, Room 1127
Washington, DC 20523

National Security Agency
College Relations Branch
Fort Meade, MD 20750

U.S. Nuclear Regulatory Commission
Division of Organization of Personnel
Resources and Employment Program Branch
Washington, DC 20555

Post Rates Commission
Administrative Office, Suite 300
Washington, DC 20268-0001

Postal Service (Contact your local postmaster)

Tennessee Valley Authority
Knoxville Office Complex
400 West Summit Hill Drive
Knoxville, TN 37902

United States Mission to the United Nations
799 United Nations Plaza
New York, NY 10017

**Department of Veterans Affairs, Health Services, and Research Administration**
The Department of Veterans Affairs (VA) is especially interested in hiring physicians, dentists, nurses, nurse anesthetists, physicians' assistants, podiatrists, optometrists, expanded-function dental auxiliaries, occupational therapists, pharmacists, licensed practical/vocational nurses, physical therapists, and certified/registered respiratory therapists. Employment inquiries should be made to one of the many VA medical centers located nationwide. Addresses and phone numbers can be found in your local area telephone directory under U.S. Government. You may also write to:

U.S. Department of Veterans Affairs
810 Vermont Avenue NW
Washington, DC 20420

**Judicial Branch**
The judicial branch of the federal government includes all legal entities except the Administrative Office of the U.S. Courts and the U.S. Claims Court. For judicial branch employment information contact:

United States Supreme Court Building Personnel Office
1 First Street NE
Washington, DC 20543

Administrative Office of the U.S. Courts
Personnel Division, Room L701
Washington, DC 20544

U.S. Claims Court
717 Madison Place NW
Washington, DC 20005

**Legislative Branch**
The legislative branch of the federal government includes senators' and representatives' offices, the Library of Congress, and the U.S. Capitol. For employment information contact:

U.S. Senate Placement Office
Senate Hart Building, Room 142B
Washington, DC 20510

U.S. House of Representatives
House Placement Office
House Office Building, Annex 2, Room 219
Third and D Street SW
Washington, DC 20515-6609
202-226-6731

Library of Congress
Employment Office
Room 107, Madison Building
Washington, DC 20540
202-707-5627

**Public International Organizations**
The United States holds membership in numerous international organizations that are not part of the federal government. For employment information and application procedures contact:

International Monetary Fund
Recruiting and Training Division
700 Nineteenth Street NW
Washington, DC 20431

Pan American Health Organization
Pan American Sanitary Bureau
Regional Office of the World Health Organizations
525 Twenty-third Street NW
Washington, DC 20037

United Nations Children's Fund
3 United States Plaza
New York, NY 10017

United Nations Development Program
1 United Nations Plaza
New York, NY 10017

United Nations Institute for Training and Research
801 United Nations Plaza
New York, NY 10017

United Nations Population Fund
220 East 42nd Street
New York, NY 10017

United Nations Secretariat
Office of Personnel Services
Recruitment Programs Section
New York, NY 10017

World Bank, IFC and MIGA
Recruitment Division, International Recruitment
1818 H Street NW
Washington, DC 20433

# THE TRAVEL INDUSTRY

Of all the industries worldwide, travel and tourism continues to grow at an astounding rate. Nearly everyone tries to take at least one vacation every year, and many people travel frequently on business. Some travel for education or for that special honeymoon or anniversary trip. And where there's travel, there are foreign languages and opportunities for those who speak more than one language. In this industry, unlike in the fields of interpreting and translating, languages are considered secondary assets—not the primary skills you would need to get hired. But secondary or not, if you don't speak another language, your chances for landing a plum travel industry job fade. Given two candidates with equal degrees, training, and qualifications, both personable, well-groomed, and people oriented, but one speaks only English and the other both English and fairly decent Spanish (or French, or Italian, or German . . .), the choice is obvious.

So, if you have adequate language skills and would love to use them in an industry that values international culture and differences, consider travel and tourism. The industry needs multilingual people to cater to foreign clients, draw up and negotiate contracts, do sales presentations in foreign languages, and communicate with international clientele. The following areas within travel and tourism can provide exciting careers for those with the necessary skills and qualifications—and language capabilities.

## HOTEL, RESORT, AND CRUISE STAFF

Hotels and resorts in areas frequented by international travelers and cruise lines with an international clientele need a variety of staff—and would prefer that staff to be bi- or multilingual. There are many different positions within hotels, resorts, and cruise lines; the following are most likely to attract candidates with foreign language skills.

## Hotel and Resort Managers

Managers are responsible for the efficient and profitable operation of their establishments. In a small hotel, motel, or inn with a limited staff, a single manager may direct all aspects of operations. However, large hotels may employ hundreds of workers, and the manager may be aided by a number of assistant managers responsible for various aspects of operations among departments. Assistant managers must see to it that the day-to-day operations of their departments meet the general manager's standards.

The general manager has overall responsibility for the operation of the hotel. Within guidelines established by the owners of the hotel or executives of the hotel chain, the general manager sets room rates, allocates funds to departments, approves expenditures, and establishes standards for service to guests, decor, housekeeping, food quality, and banquet operations.

Resident managers live in hotels and are on call twenty-four hours a day to resolve any problems or emergencies, although they normally work an eight-hour day. As the most senior assistant manager, a resident manager oversees the day-to-day operations of the hotel. In many hotels, the general manager also serves as the resident manager.

Front office managers coordinate reservations and room assignments and train and direct the hotel's front desk staff, which deals with the public. They ensure that guests are handled courteously and efficiently, complaints and problems are resolved, and requests for special services are carried out.

Food and beverage managers direct the food services of hotels, overseeing the operation of hotels' restaurants, cocktail lounges, and banquet facilities. They supervise and schedule food and beverage preparation, supervise service workers, plan menus, estimate costs, and deal with food suppliers as well as customers.

Convention services managers coordinate the activities of large hotels' various departments for meetings, conventions, and other special events. They meet with representatives of groups or organizations to plan the number of rooms to reserve, the desired configuration of hotel meeting space, and any banquet services needed. During the meeting or event, they resolve unexpected problems and monitor activities to check that hotel operations conform to the expectations of the group.

Other assistant managers may be specialists responsible for activities such as personnel, accounting and office administration, marketing and sales, purchasing, security, maintenance, and recreational facilities.

## Cruise Staff

Probably everyone, at one time or another, has seen reruns of "The Love Boat" on television and watched Julie, Doc, Isaac, Gopher, and Captain Stubing go about their daily activities, interacting with passengers while ensuring everyone has the best vacation ever. Although the series might not exactly mirror reality, being part of a cruise ship staff can be fun and exciting, with the opportunity to travel to exotic ports, meet all different kinds of people, make new friends, and lead a carefree lifestyle.

Cruise lines employ all sorts of personnel to handle the many tasks involved with running a ship. A smaller ship with 850 passengers might have over 400 crew members; larger ships that carry 2,500 or so passengers employ up to 1,000 crew members. The "marine crew"—the captain, seamen, deck officers, oilers, and engineering officers—generally come from the ship's country of origin. Most of the jobs open to Americans are as part of the "hotel crew."

To fully understand what a cruise ship is like, think of it as a hotel that floats. Just as hotels have different personalities and amenities, so do cruises. Some are deluxe, offering the best food and service, as would an elegant hotel. Other cruises are more casual and fun, filled with activities that cater to a young crowd. Whatever style the cruise, most employ crews to work in the following positions:

| | | |
|---|---|---|
| Accountant | Doctor/Nurse | Reservationist |
| Assistant Cruise Director | Entertainer | Sales Manager |
| Beautician | Gift Shop Manager/ | Shore Excursions Director |
| Casino Operator | Assistant | Sports/Fitness Director |
| Cruise Director | Photographer | Stewards |
| Cruise Staff/Activities | Port Lecturer | Waiters/Waitresses |
| Disc Jockey | Purser | Youth Counselor |

Job titles and responsibilities vary from ship to ship. Cruise staff put in long hours—anywhere from eight to fifteen hours a day, seven days a week—and must maintain a high level of energy and always be cordial and friendly to the passengers.

When in port, most of the crew are allowed to go ashore and have time off to explore, although some cruise staff function as chaperones, helping passengers find their way around foreign locales. Shipboard activities usually follow a rigid schedule, with little time in between for the crew to take a break. With a constant eye on their watches, cruise staff run from one activity to another, announcing games over the loudspeaker, setting up the deck for exercise classes, supervising ring-toss tournaments or other special events, and encouraging everyone to participate.

An outgoing, energetic individual would be in his element in such a job; someone lacking those skills would find the work very difficult.

## Salaries for Hotel Personnel

Median annual earnings of hotel managers and assistants were $26,700 in 1998. The middle 50 percent of these workers earned between $19,820 and $34,690. The lowest 10 percent had earnings of less than $14,430, while the top 10 percent earned over $45,520. In 1997, median annual earnings in the lodging industry, where nearly all of these workers are employed, were $28,600.

Salaries of hotel managers and assistants vary greatly according to their responsibilities and the segment of the hotel industry in which they are employed. Managers in some hotels may earn bonuses up to 25 percent of their basic salary and may also be furnished with lodging, meals, parking, laundry, and other services. In addition to typical benefits, some hotels offer profit-sharing plans and educational assistance to their employees.

Earnings of hotel, motel, and resort desk clerks also vary considerably depending on the location, size, and type of establishment in which they work. For example, clerks at large luxury hotels and those located in metropolitan and resort areas generally pay clerks more than less-exclusive or "budget" establishments and those located in less-populated areas. In addition to their hourly wage, full-time information clerks who work evenings, nights, weekends, or holidays may receive shift differential pay.

## Salaries for Cruise Staff

While salaries are not overly generous, the additional benefits are. Cruise staff are provided with free food and housing while shipboard. It's not necessary for a full-time employee of a cruise line to maintain quarters ashore, and therefore most of the salary can be saved. Cruise ships also sail to exotic ports, giving staff members the chance to travel and meet people from all over the world.

## Training for Hotel Personnel

At many hotels, on-the-job training is possible at all levels of employment, but completing a formal training program will help you compete. Without experience, you might very well get hired but start at the bottom of the ladder. With a college degree in hotel management or a related field, you could walk into an assistant manager position or be offered a place in a management training program.

In the past, most managers were promoted from the ranks of front desk clerks, housekeepers, waiters, chefs, and hotel sales workers. Although some people still advance to hotel management positions without the benefit of education or training beyond high school, postsecondary education is increasingly important. A bachelor's degree in hotel and restaurant administration provides particularly strong preparation for a career in hotel management, although a college liberal arts degree may be sufficient when coupled with related hotel experience.

Restaurant management training or experience is a good background for entering hotel management because the success of a hotel's food service and beverage operations is often of great importance to the profitability of the entire establishment.

More than 160 colleges and universities offer bachelor's and graduate programs in this field. More than 800 community and junior colleges, technical institutes, vocational and trade schools, and other academic institutions also have programs leading to an associate degree or other formal recognition in hotel or restaurant management. Graduates of hotel or restaurant management programs usually start as trainee assistant managers, or at least advance to such positions more quickly.

Hotel management programs usually include instruction in hotel administration, accounting, economics, marketing, housekeeping, food service management and catering, hotel maintenance engineering, and data processing—reflecting the widespread use of computers in hotel operations such as reservations, accounting, and housekeeping management. Programs encourage part-time or summer work in hotels and restaurants because the experience gained and the contacts made with employers may benefit students when they seek full-time employment after graduation.

**Training for Cruise Staff**  A college education is not necessary, but some cruise lines prefer to see an applicant with a degree in psychology, hotel management, physical education, or communications. It's also a good idea to know another language, especially Spanish or German. Equally important are the following personal qualities:

- Patience

- Diplomacy

- Tolerance for a wide variety of people

- A never-ending supply of energy

- An outgoing and genuinely friendly nature

- Enthusiasm

- Artistic talent

- Athletic ability

Most successful applicants land their jobs by applying directly to the various cruise lines, which are located mainly in Miami, Fort Lauderdale, Los Angeles, San Francisco, and New York. Look through the Yellow Pages for each city for cruise line addresses and phone numbers.

## RESTAURANT MANAGEMENT AND STAFF

Independent restaurants or restaurants in airports, hotels, and resorts frequented by international travelers benefit from a staff that can communicate in more than one language. Positions with the greatest need for additional languages include:

Bartenders
Managers
Wait Staff

In addition, American fast-food chains and restaurants such as McDonald's and Pizza Hut are springing up all over the globe. Restaurant managers with language skills are desperately needed to set up these enterprises.

**Managers**

The daily responsibilities of many restaurant and food service managers can be as complicated as a meal prepared by a fine chef. In addition to the traditional duties of selecting and pricing menu items, using food and other supplies efficiently, and achieving quality in food preparation and service, managers are now responsible for a growing number of administrative and human resource tasks. For example, they must carefully find and evaluate new ways of recruiting employees in a tight job market. Once hired, managers must also find creative ways to retain experienced workers.

In most restaurants and institutional food service facilities, the manager is assisted in these duties by one or more assistant managers, depending on the size and operating hours of the establishment. In most large establishments, as well as in many smaller ones, the management team consists of a general manager, one or more assistant managers, and an executive chef. The executive chef is responsible for the operation of the kitchen, while the assistant managers oversee service in the dining room and other areas. In smaller restaurants, the executive chef also may be the general manager and sometimes an owner. In fast-food restaurants and other food service facilities open for long hours, often seven days a week, the manager is aided by several assistant managers, each of whom supervises a shift of workers.

The quality of food and services in restaurants depends largely on a manager's ability to interview, hire, and, when necessary, fire employees. This is especially true in tight labor markets, when many managers report difficulty in hiring experienced food and beverage preparation and service workers. Managers may attend career fairs or arrange for newspaper advertising to expand their pool of applicants. Once a new employee is hired, managers explain the establishment's policies and practices and oversee any necessary training. Managers also schedule the work hours of employees, making sure there are enough workers to cover peak dining periods. If employees are unable to work, managers may have to fill in for them. Some managers regularly help with cooking, clearing of tables, or other tasks.

Another fundamental responsibility of restaurant and food service managers is supervising the kitchen and dining room. For example, managers often oversee all food preparation and cooking, examining the quality and portion sizes to ensure that dishes are prepared and garnished correctly and in a timely manner. They also investigate and resolve customers' complaints about food quality or service. In an international setting, it is important to know more than one language.

**Wait Staff and Bartenders**

Whether they work in small, informal diners or large, elegant restaurants, all food and beverage service workers aim to help customers have a positive dining experience. These workers are responsible for greeting customers (perhaps using a language other than English), taking food and drink orders, serving food, cleaning up after patrons, and preparing tables and dining areas. All of these duties require a high quality of service so customers will return.

Bartenders fill the drink orders that waiters and waitresses take from customers. They prepare standard mixed drinks and, occasionally, are asked to mix drinks to suit a customer's taste. Most bartenders know dozens of drink recipes and can mix drinks accurately, quickly, and without waste, even during the busiest periods. Bartenders also collect payment, operate the cash register, clean up after customers leave, and often serve food to customers seated at the bar. Bartenders also check identification of customers seated at the bar to ensure they meet the minimum age requirement for the purchase of alcohol and tobacco products. The majority of bartenders who work in eating and drinking establishments directly serve and interact with patrons. Because customers typically frequent drinking establishments for the friendly atmosphere, most bartenders must be friendly and helpful with customers.

Food and beverage service workers are on their feet most of the time and often carry heavy trays of food, dishes, and glassware. During busy dining periods, they are under pressure to serve customers quickly and efficiently. Part-time work is more common among food and beverage service workers than among workers in almost any other occupation. Those on part-time schedules include half of all waiters and waitresses and six out of ten food counter and fountain workers, compared to one out of six workers throughout the economy. Slightly more than half of all bartenders work full time, with 35 percent working part time and the remainder working a variable schedule.

## Training for Restaurant Managers

Most food service management companies and national or regional restaurant chains recruit management trainees from two- and four-year college hospitality management programs. Food service and restaurant chains prefer to hire people with degrees in restaurant and institutional food service management, but they often hire graduates with degrees in other fields who have demonstrated interest and aptitude. Some restaurant and food service manager positions, particularly in self-service and fast-food restaurants, are filled by promoting experienced food and beverage preparation and service workers. Waiters, waitresses, chefs, and fast-food workers demonstrating potential for handling increased responsibility sometimes advance to assistant manager or management trainee jobs.

A bachelor's degree in restaurant and food service management provides a particularly strong preparation for a career in this occupation. In 1998, more than 150 colleges and universities offered four-year programs in restaurant and hotel management or institutional food service management. For those not interested in pursuing a four-year degree, more than 800 community and junior colleges, technical institutes, and other institutions offer programs in these fields leading to an associate's degree or other formal certification.

Most employers emphasize personal qualities when hiring managers. Self-discipline, initiative, and leadership ability are essential. Managers must be able to solve problems and concentrate on details. They need good communication skills to deal with customers and suppliers, as well as to motivate and direct their staff.

Most restaurant chains and food service management companies have rigorous training programs for management positions. Through a combination of classroom and on-the-job training, trainees receive instruction and gain work experience in all aspects of the operations of a restaurant or institutional food service facility. Topics include food preparation, nutrition, sanitation, security, company policies and procedures, personnel management, record keeping, and preparation of reports. Training to use the restaurant's computer system is increasingly important as well. After six months to a year, trainees usually receive their first permanent assignment as an assistant manager.

Willingness to relocate often is essential for advancement to positions with greater responsibility. Managers typically advance to larger establishments or regional management positions within restaurant chains. Some eventually open their own eating and drinking establishments. Others transfer to hotel management positions because their restaurant management experience is a good background for food and beverage manager jobs in hotels and resorts.

## Training for Wait Staff and Bartenders

There are no specific educational requirements for food and beverage service jobs. Although many employers prefer to hire high school graduates as wait staff and bartenders, completion of high school is usually not required for fast-food workers, counter attendants, dining room attendants, and bartender helpers.

For many people, a job as a food and beverage service worker serves as a source of immediate income rather than as a career. Many entrants to these jobs are in their late teens or early twenties and have a high school education or less. Usually, they have little or no work experience. Many are full-time students or homemakers. Food and beverage service jobs are a major source of part-time employment for high school and college students.

Because maintaining a restaurant's image is important to its success, employers emphasize personal qualities. Food and beverage service workers are in close contact with the public, so these workers should be well-spoken and have a neat, clean appearance. They should enjoy dealing with all kinds of people and possess a pleasant disposition.

Usually, bartenders must be at least twenty-one years of age, but employers prefer to hire people who are twenty-five or older. Bartenders should be familiar with state and local laws concerning the sale of alcoholic beverages.

Most food and beverage service workers pick up their skills on the job by observing and working with more-experienced workers. Some employers, particularly those in fast-food restaurants, use self-instruction programs with audio-visual presentations and instructional booklets to teach new employees food preparation and service skills. Some public and private vocational schools, restaurant associations, and large restaurant chains provide classroom training in a generalized food service curriculum. Some bartenders acquire their skills by attending a bartending or vocational and technical school. These programs often include instruction on state and local laws and regulations, cocktail recipes, attire and conduct, and stocking a bar. Some of these schools help their graduates find jobs.

## Salaries

Median earnings of food service managers were $26,700 in 1998. The middle 50 percent earned between $19,820 and $34,690. The lowest-paid 10 percent earned $14,430 or less, while the highest-paid 10 percent earned over $45,520. In addition to typical benefits, most salaried restaurant and food service managers receive free meals and, depending on their length of service, the opportunity for additional training.

Food and beverage service workers derive their earnings from a combination of hourly wages and customer tips. Earnings vary greatly depending on the type of job and establishment. In some restaurants, these workers contribute a portion of their tips to a tip pool, which is distributed among the establishment's other food and beverage service workers and kitchen staff. Tip pools allow workers who normally do not receive tips, such as dining room attendants, to share in the rewards of a well-served meal.

In 1998, median hourly earnings (not including tips) of full-time waiters and waitresses were $5.85. The middle 50 percent earned between $5.58 and $6.32; the top 10 percent earned at least $7.83. For most waiters and waitresses, higher earnings are primarily the result of receiving more in tips rather than higher hourly wages. Tips usually average between 10 and 20 percent of guests' checks, so waiters and waitresses working in busy, expensive restaurants earn the most.

Full-time bartenders had median hourly earnings (not including tips) of $6.25 in 1998. The middle 50 percent earned between $5.72 and $7.71; the top 10 percent earned at least $9.19 an hour. Like waiters and waitresses, bartenders employed in public bars may receive more than half of their earnings as tips. Service bartenders are often paid higher hourly wages to offset their lower tip earnings.

## TRAVEL AGENTS

Travel agencies hire people who speak foreign languages to answer phones and deal with customers from other countries.

Travel agents generally work in an office and deal with customers in person or over the phone. They plot itineraries, make airline and hotel reservations, book passage on cruise ships, or arrange for car rentals. They work with affluent, sophisticated travelers or first-timers such as students trying to travel on a budget. They may book a simple, round-trip air ticket for a person traveling alone or handle arrangements for hundreds of people traveling to attend a convention or conference. Some travel agents are generalists; they handle all situations. Others specialize in a particular area, such as cruises or corporate travel.

Travel agents gather information from different sources. They use computer databases, attend trade shows, and read trade magazines. They also visit resorts or locations to get firsthand knowledge about a destination. The field offers wonderful opportunities throughout the year for free travel on "fam" (familiarity) trips.

Travel agents work hard, though. They have to keep up with rapidly changing fares and rates, and they have to know who offers the best packages and service. The downside, according to many travel agents, is that they seldom have enough free time to do all the traveling they would like. They are often tied to their desks, especially during peak travel periods such as the summer or important holidays.

**Salaries for Travel Agents**

Salary varies according to the region in which you work and your experience. Depending on the agency, you could start out on an hourly wage or a yearly salary. Some travel agents prefer to work on a commission basis. That way, the more trips they sell, the more money they earn. A salary plus commission is ideal. Travel agents who are good salespeople can also earn bonuses or more free or discounted trips. If your pay is initially low, it can be offset by this added benefit.

**Training for Travel Agents**

A four-year college degree is not necessary to become a travel agent. It can be helpful, however, and shows commitment and discipline. Most travel agents study for at least two years and earn an associate degree. Many community colleges, and trade and vocational schools offer good programs in travel and tourism or hospitality management. Some travel agencies are willing to hire and train inexperienced applicants.

For a list of schools offering certified programs, write to the American Society of Travel Agents or the Institute of Certified Travel Agents. (Their addresses are listed at the end of this chapter.)

## AIRLINE AND AIRPORT PERSONNEL

Airlines and airports employ people with additional language skills in a variety of capacities, particularly as reservation and ticket clerks and flight attendants. (Pilots and air traffic controllers do not need to know another language; their work is conducted solely in English.)

Customs officials and immigration officials usually need to know more than one language. See Chapter 5 for more information on these careers.

**Reservation Clerks and Ticket Agents**

Many travelers rely on the services of reservation clerks and ticket agents. These people perform functions as varied as selling tickets, confirming reservations, checking baggage, and providing tourists with useful travel information. Most of them work for airlines, usually in large reservation centers answering telephone inquiries and offering suggestions on travel arrangements, such as routes, time schedules, rates, and types of accommodation.

Reservation agents quote fares, provide travel information, and make and confirm transportation reservations. Transportation ticket agents are sometimes known as passenger service agents, passenger-booking clerks, reservation clerks, airport service agents, ticket clerks, or ticket sellers. They work in train and bus stations as well as airports selling tickets, assigning seats to passengers, and checking baggage. In addition, they may answer inquiries and give directions, examine passports and visas, or check in pets.

Other ticket agents commonly known as gate or station agents work in airport terminals assisting passengers boarding airplanes. These workers direct passengers to the correct boarding area, check tickets and seat assignments, make boarding announcements, and provide special assistance to young, elderly, or disabled passengers when they board or disembark. Training is usually on the job.

Employment of reservation and transportation ticket agents is sensitive to cyclical swings in the economy. During recessions, discretionary passenger travel declines, and transportation service companies are less likely to hire new workers and may even resort to layoffs.

## Salaries for Reservation and Transportation Ticket Agents

Reservation and transportation ticket agents currently earn an average yearly salary of $22,120. They receive free or reduced-rate travel on their company's carriers for themselves and their immediate family and, in some companies, for friends.

## Flight Attendants

Major airlines are required by law to provide flight attendants for the safety of the flying public. Although the primary job of the flight attendants is to ensure that safety regulations are adhered to, they also try to make flights comfortable and enjoyable for passengers.

At least one hour before each flight, flight attendants are briefed by the captain (the pilot in command) on such things as emergency evacuation procedures, crew coordination, length of flight, expected weather conditions, and special passenger problems. Flight attendants make sure that first aid kits and other emergency equipment are aboard and in working order and that the passenger cabin is in order, with adequate supplies of food, beverages, and blankets. As passengers board the plane, flight attendants greet them, check their tickets, and instruct them on where to store coats and carry-on items.

Before the plane takes off, flight attendants instruct all passengers in the use of emergency equipment and check to see that seat belts are fastened, seat backs are in upright positions, and all carry-on items are properly stowed. In the air, helping passengers in the event of an emergency is the most important responsibility of a flight attendant.

Safety-related actions may range from reassuring passengers during occasional encounters with strong turbulence to directing passengers who must evacuate a plane following an emergency landing. Flight attendants also answer questions about the flight; distribute reading material, pillows, and blankets; and help small children, elderly or disabled people, and any others needing assistance. They may also administer first aid to passengers who become ill.

Flight attendants generally serve beverages and other refreshments and, on many flights, heat and distribute precooked meals or snacks. After the plane has landed, flight attendants take inventory of headsets, alcoholic beverages, and moneys collected. They also report any medical problems passengers may have had and the condition of cabin equipment.

Lead, or first, flight attendants, sometimes known as pursers, oversee the work of the other attendants aboard the aircraft while performing most of the same duties.

Because airlines operate around the clock year-round, flight attendants may work nights, holidays, and weekends. They usually fly seventy-five to eighty hours a month and in addition spend an equal amount of time each month on the ground preparing planes for flights, writing reports following completed flights, and waiting for planes to arrive. Because of variations in scheduling and limitations on flying time, many flight attendants have eleven or more days off each month. They may be away from their home base at least one-third of the time. During this period, the airlines provide hotel accommodations and an allowance for meal expenses.

The combination of free time and discount airfares gives flight attendants the opportunity to travel and see new places. However, the work can be strenuous and trying. Short flights require speedy service if meals are served, and turbulent flights can make serving drinks and meals difficult. Flight attendants stand during much of the flight and must remain pleasant and efficient regardless of how tired they are or how demanding passengers may be. Occasionally, they must deal with disruptive passengers.

## Training for Flight Attendants

Airlines prefer to hire poised, tactful, and resourceful people who can interact comfortably with strangers and remain calm under stress. Applicants usually must be at least eighteen to twenty-one years old. Flight attendants must have excellent health and the ability to speak clearly. In addition, there generally are height requirements, and most airlines want candidates with weight proportionate to height. Prospective flight attendants usually must be willing to relocate, although some flight attendants are able to commute to and from their home base.

Applicants must be high school graduates. Those having several years of college or experience in dealing with the public are preferred. More and more flight attendants being hired are college graduates. Highly desirable areas of concentration include such people-oriented disciplines as psychology and education.

Flight attendants for international airlines generally must speak an appropriate foreign language fluently. Some of the major airlines prefer candidates who can speak two major foreign languages for their international flights.

Once hired, candidates must undergo a period of training. The length of training depends on the size and type of carrier, ranging from four to seven weeks, and takes place in the airline's flight training center. Airlines that do not operate training centers generally send new employees to another airline's center. Airlines may provide transportation to the training centers and an allowance for room and board and school supplies. However, new trainees are not considered employees of the airline until they successfully complete the training program. Some airlines may actually charge individuals for training.

Trainees learn emergency procedures such as evacuating an airplane, operating emergency systems and equipment, administering first aid, and using water survival tactics. In addition, trainees are taught how to deal with disruptive passengers and hijacking and terrorist situations. New hires learn flight regulations and duties, company operations and policies, and receive instruction on personal grooming and weight control. Trainees for the international routes get additional instruction in passport and customs regulations. Toward the end of their training, students go on practice flights. Additionally, flight attendants must receive twelve to fourteen hours of annual training in emergency procedures and passenger relations.

After completing initial training, flight attendants are assigned to one of their airline's bases. New flight attendants are placed on "reserve status" and are called on to either staff extra flights or fill in for crew members who are sick, on vacation, or rerouted. When not on duty, reserve flight attendants must be available to report for flights on short notice. They usually remain on reserve for at least one year, but in some cities it may take five to ten years or longer to advance from reserve status.

Flight attendants who no longer are on reserve bid monthly for regular assignments. Because assignments are based on seniority, usually only the most experienced attendants get their choice of assignments.

Advancement takes longer today than in the past because experienced flight attendants are remaining in this career longer than they used to. Some flight attendants become supervisors or take on additional duties such as recruiting and instructing.

## Salaries for Flight Attendants

According to data from the Association of Flight Attendants, beginning flight attendants had median earnings of about $13,700 a year in 1998. Flight attendants with six years of experience had median annual earnings of about $20,000, while some senior flight attendants earned as much as $50,000 a year.

Beginning pay scales for flight attendants vary by carrier. New hires usually begin at the same pay scale regardless of experience, and all flight attendants receive the same future pay increases.

Flight attendants receive extra compensation for night and international flights and for increased hours. In addition, some airlines offer incentive pay for working holidays or taking positions that require additional responsibility or paperwork. Most airlines guarantee a minimum of sixty-five to seventy-five flight hours per month, with the option to work additional hours. Flight attendants also receive a per diem allowance for meal expenses while on duty away from home. In addition, flight attendants and their immediate families are entitled to free fares on their own airline and reduced fares on most other airlines.

Flight attendants are required to purchase uniforms and wear them while on duty. The airlines usually pay for uniform replacement items and may provide a small allowance to cover cleaning and upkeep of the uniforms.

## TOUR GUIDES

Whether leading a group on a bus tour of New York or heading a boat tour through the canals of Venice, tour guides come into contact with visitors from every country. English is the international language, of course, and most people outside of English-speaking countries who study another language opt to add English to their repertoire, but just as many know only their own language. Most tourist attractions these days offer recorded tours on CDs in a variety of languages. But a tour guide who can communicate in a variety of languages will be very successful and much appreciated.

**What a Tour Guide Does**

Tour guides may work with one particular group for an extended period of time—for example, chaperoning a school group through Europe for a month—or with a variety of people throughout the day—providing information on historic cathedrals or castles, for example, or pointing out sites of interest as their bus or boat passes by. They may also lead walking tours, showing a group around particular neighborhoods or districts.

**Becoming a Tour Guide**

Most tour guides are taught on the job. Through printed material, the information passed on by other guides, and their own research, they learn enough about a particular attraction or area to answer questions.

Some tour guides start off as volunteers, in museums, for example. Others are hired directly by a tour company and are paid a salary or commission based on the number of people in a tour group.

## FIRSTHAND ACCOUNTS

### Mary Fallon Miller
### Travel Agent

Mary Fallon Miller started her career as a travel agent in 1986, when she opened her own agency. In partnership with a relative, she first focused on bus tours, transporting groups to see special events in her area. She later moved on to specialize in cruise travel.

**Getting Started**

"At the age of seven, I sailed across the Atlantic on the S.S. *France*, and as a young woman, I accompanied my mother throughout Europe and South

America. I fell in love with the glamour and excitement of travel. It gets in your blood; I have a real fascination for other cultures and languages. I realized that a career as a travel agent would allow me to pursue my dream to see more of the world."

**What the Work Is Really Like**

"When you're just starting out, you're tied to the office and the computer a lot, but a newcomer would get to take at least one week a year, more once you've gained some seniority. The owners of a travel agency get to go on more 'fam' trips, but if someone just starting out is seen as a productive member of the business, helping to build it, he or she would get more opportunities. You'll be the one they send on the 'Cruise-a-Thon' or to the ski shows, and then you'll become your agency's representative.

"Beginners would probably start working side by side with someone more experienced in the agency. They might be placed in a specific department handling, for example, European travel, cruises, or car rentals and airfares. Much of their time will be spent coordinating and arranging details.

"It can be tricky keeping all the details accurate and being able to deal with what we call 'grumps and whiners.' There are people who get very nervous about their travel arrangements, and they can complain and make your life miserable. But you have to be able to be compassionate—find out why they're so concerned. Maybe they had a bad experience in the past. You have to learn as much about your client as possible.

"And there are times when things go wrong. There could be a snow-in at an airport and people miss their connections, or someone in the family dies and they have to cancel their whole cruise reservation at the last minute. You have to be professional and flexible, and you have to be on the ball all the time.

"It's a demanding job, but it's satisfying. People come back and say, 'I can't believe you knew exactly what I wanted. That's the best vacation I've ever had. And I'm telling all my friends.' You start getting more and more customers coming in, and they ask for you by name. That feels really good. You're making a dream come true, and in a way, that's what you're doing—selling dreams."

**Advice from Mary Fallon Miller**

"Read *Time*, *Newsweek*, and your local newspaper. Try to stay in touch with the world. Listen to National Public Radio or watch the travel channel on television. Don't be afraid of learning the computer. Study languages and, if you have the chance, participate in a language club or take advantage of a foreign exchange program. I lived in Poland for a summer. Most important, learn communication skills.

"And, at the beginning, when you're doing some of the drudgery work, it helps to remember that down the road you will receive discounts and free travel, that you are working toward something. The hard work will pay off."

### Joanne Leon
### Assistant Director of Sales

Joanne Leon has been in the hotel and sales business for twenty years. She works at a well-known national chain hotel. In her particular property in Miami, Florida, she is responsible for 207 suites and three meeting rooms.

**Getting Started**

"Right out of high school I worked for a chamber of commerce, for the convention and sales department. That's where I first got into the convention end. I got to see how they booked the whole city, how they go after major conventions. I worked with booking blocks of hotel rooms citywide, versus working in one specific hotel. After about a year there, I realized I wouldn't have a chance for advancement. Hotels offer better opportunities and more money. The experience I got with the chamber of commerce translated well into hotel work.

"I took a position as a sales and catering secretary at a hotel chain in Oregon. They had about seventy-five very upscale hotels. I was there only six months and learned everything I could. Then I applied for a position in another hotel that I saw was under construction about two hours away. I sat with the general manager in the coffee shop for an hour or so. He ended up calling me and offering me the sales and convention manager position. It was on a trial basis because of my age; I was only twenty at the time. The drinking age was twenty-one, so they had legal issues to deal with about my selling liquor. That was a great job. They could seat a thousand and I pretty much ran all of that. I stayed there for three and a half years, but then an opportunity came up for me to go back to the first Oregon hotel as the sales and catering manager. It turned out to be a good move for me, more money, more knowledge. After three years I moved south, to Alabama, but there weren't as many hotel opportunities there for me, so I went into the legal field for a while and worked as a legal secretary. But I missed the hotels. It's usually something you either love or hate, there's no in between. I finally found a job in Mobile and traveled between five different states promoting the hotel.

"In 1990 I started here in Miami. My first position was as sales and catering manager, and later I moved up to my current position, assistant director of sales. The next step up for me would be director of sales, then I could even think about moving into a general manager position. The opportunities are there, and they're willing to train you."

**What the Work Is Like**

"Every day is different, not like in some jobs where the work can get monotonous. The hotel industry isn't like that. You might come in in the morning with a plan to work on something specific, then something comes up and you end up doing something else. The meeting planners for a large group convention might come in and want to discuss details with you, so you put your other work on hold for a while.

"Basically, the way it works in the sales end of things is that you're out looking for new business and staying on top of your current business. We look for corporate customers, and we want to stay in touch on a regular basis.

"I'm on the phone a lot, checking details, taking care of rooming lists. There are always a lot of details and you have to follow through on promises you make. For example, if you promised to hold ten two-bedded suites for them, you have to make sure that's what got booked, not ten king suites. And with conferences, you need to follow up on audiovisual equipment or registration tables, that sort of thing. I'm up and down a lot, too; I'm not just always sitting at a desk. I walk around the hotel, double-check on my groups, make sure they're happy. As I said, every day is new because you're working with different people all the time. That's what I think makes it fun.

"But, as with any job, there are always some downsides. Sometimes you get bogged down with paperwork, but if you're an organized person, you should be able to stay on top of it. It's not too bad. Another thing in this business, a hotel never closes, so your hours won't always be the best sometimes. You could be working nights, weekends. However, I think once you put in enough time, you can move into some of the positions in which you don't have such a messed up schedule. With a smaller hotel, it's a little easier.

"The advantages far outweigh the disadvantages. In sales you're working with some high-energy people in an up kind of atmosphere. We have bells on our desks and when we book something we ring our bells. We laugh and have a good time at our job. It's fun to go to work. I've never gotten up in the morning and dreaded going in."

**Advice from Joanne Leon**

"If you're going to be in this industry, you have to be a people person and have a happy personality. You have to be able to always have a smile on your face, and if a guest or a customer is dissatisfied, you have to be able to handle it. You don't ever want to lose business. You have to be a team player, too. If the restaurant gets busy, for example, I'll go over and help them out there. If someone needs help, then that's what you do. Our job descriptions aren't rigidly set. But it's fun to do something different once in a while.

"Miami is in a cosmopolitan area, and a lot of our customers speak a language other than English. I know a little Spanish, and I am taking a night class in German. It really makes a difference if you can exchange even a few words in the customers' native language. They appreciate your effort.

"Another thing, when you're looking for work, you'll probably be better off working for a corporate-owned hotel rather than a family-owned franchise. There'll be more opportunities for you to move up and probably better salaries. But don't get discouraged when you're starting out at the bottom. A position at the front desk might not be the highest-paying job, but it's a good way to learn."

### Richard Turnwald
### Chief Purser

Richard Turnwald has been working in the cruise industry for more than sixteen years. He started out shoreside in the operations department, where he handled everything from personnel to ordering supplies for the ships. He went from there to positions with the cruise staff as a shore excursions director, assistant cruise director, and port lecturer providing information on the different ports of call. He then worked his way up the ranks from junior purser to chief purser.

**Getting Started**

"Ever since I was a little boy, I've always loved ships and the sea. I read about them and studied them, and there was no doubt in my mind that I wanted to be involved in some way with ships as a profession. Later, I was in college in Michigan studying travel and tourism, and I wanted to get involved with the cruise lines. I sent out my résumé and wrote to the various cruise lines, most of which were based in Miami. I was interviewed over the telephone and offered a position in the office. It was exciting and scary at the same time. I was just out of college and I had to relocate to a place where I didn't know anyone, but it was like a dream for me to finally be able to work closely with the cruise ships."

**What the Work Is Like**

"The purser's office is like the front desk at a big hotel. The staff handle all the money on the ship, pay all the bills and the salaries, cash traveler's checks for passengers, provide the safes for the valuables, fill out all the documentation for customs and immigration officials in the different countries, and all the other crucial behind-the-scenes functions. The purser is the one who passengers come to for information or help with problems. Pursers are in charge of cabin assignments, and they also coordinate with the medical personnel to help handle any emergencies.

"There are various ranks for a purser: junior or assistant purser, second purser, first purser, then chief purser. As chief purser I am responsible for a staff of six people; on larger ships the purser's office might have fourteen or fifteen people.

"Promotions are based on your ability, how well you do your job, as well as the length of time you've been employed. I was fortunate; I rose up through the ranks fairly quickly. Within three months I had worked my way up from junior purser to chief purser. But that's really an exceptional situation. It usually takes a good year or so. It depends on how many people are ahead of you, if they leave or stay. It can be very competitive. You have to consider that there's only one chief purser on each ship. Some people start working on a ship and their only background is watching "The Love Boat" and thinking from that how wonderful it would be. They don't have a realistic viewpoint of the downsides of cruise work."

**The Upsides and Downsides**

"When you live and work on a ship, you're an employee, you're not there to be a passenger. The living conditions are not as luxurious as for the passengers. You might be sharing a room with one or two other crew members, and there's not a lot of privacy. The food isn't as high class; passengers might be having lobster and steak upstairs while the crew are eating fish or meatloaf below. You might be away from home for the first time and feeling homesick and cut off.

"There's a sense of confinement on a ship; you can't just go out to dinner whenever you want. Cabin fever is common. You live your job twenty-four hours a day, and there's no getting away from that. You're on duty seven days a week, and you don't have a day off for several months at a time. Some people get burned out on that, while others thrive.

"If you take a positive approach, you realize that you don't have to commute to work or worry about housing. Though you don't get an entire day off, you get several hours at a time when you're in port to see a lot of wonderful things. I've been all over the world, to places I wouldn't have had the time or money to get to otherwise. I've been to the Caribbean, Alaska, South America, Antarctica, Europe, Hawaii. If you're on an itinerary that repeats every week, you get to know that place and its people very well, so that's a plus. And there's something so relaxing and peaceful about being at sea, just to stand by the railing of the deck and see the changes in the weather and the whales and other sea life. Another advantage is the money. You work hard and very intensely for long periods of time, but typically you're paid very well and it's a good opportunity to save money. I was able to buy a house."

**Advice from Richard Turnwald**

"Work on people skills, being friendly, being helpful and courteous. It's very important—you'll be representing the cruise line to a lot of people.

"You have to be willing and able to accept orders. It isn't as strict as the navy, but when you're on a ship you have to follow a lot of rules and guidelines. You've heard the expression 'to run a tight ship' . . . you have to have regulations to do that. If you're too independent-minded and don't like to be told what to do, then ship life isn't for you."

## Andrea Gleason
## Flight Attendant

Andrea was a flight attendant for more than a dozen years. She's worked on domestic as well as international flights for a major airline. She has now left the industry to raise her family.

**Getting Started**

"I did this on a bet. Way back when, my brother-in-law told me that America West was hiring, so I called them up. I interviewed three or four times, and I ended up getting the job. The first interview was a group interview with about thirty other applicants. You had to get up and talk about yourself and say what you were doing at that time. Then it went to a smaller group interview and they gave you little assignments to do. What if such and such happened, what would you do? That sort of thing. Then it went to a one-on-one interview. I got the job.

"At America West at the time, we were what they called cross-utilized. That meant that not only were we flight attendants, we also worked reservations, the ticket counter at the gate, and down at the ramp. You were never just flying. Three days a week I'd fly, the other days I'd be at the gate or whatever. I also went into the training department for a while and taught reservation clerks. Later I moved across the country and went to work for an airline based on the east coast. I flew full time then; cross-utilizations had become defunct. But every once in a while I did go off the line and do in-flight training for attendants. When I started my own training, the program was three months long because we had to learn everything. Now, for flight attendants it's just four weeks long."

**What the Work Is Like**

"The work is exhausting—you're on your feet a lot, you have very strange hours. The time differences really affect you. At first, I flew to Chicago and Newark and my overnights were in San Diego. Then I flew from New York to London and New York to Paris.

"When you do international flights, it's not required that you know another language, but it's preferred. They try to schedule it so there's someone bilingual on every flight. I do know French, so I usually got the Paris run more often than the London one.

"Our primary role is safety; secondary is service. We see ourselves as the most important safety feature on the aircraft. That's because of our knowledge of how to get out and what to do in an emergency. But a lot of the passengers are only thinking about getting their Cokes. If they don't get it as soon as they want it, they think their lives are over. They don't look at us as the people who will save them if anything should happen. But being in the transportation business, you really have to play up the service part of it.

"During takeoff we're very busy. Probably the most exhausting part of the flight is just getting everybody on. I try to remember that when I have more than one hundred people on my flight, they're not all on vacation. Some are going for work, some have just lost somebody near to them. Or they just lost the biggest deal of their life or they're going to present the biggest deal of their life. And they're all sitting in this tiny little tube together, and the emotions are just running the gamut. Add the fear of flying to that. It's not routine for them; there is stress and a lot of nerves.

"Dealing with the passengers can be the hardest part. On a recent flight, even before we left I had a passenger who was back in the bathroom smoking. One of the other flight attendants said something to her about it, but she denied it. Later on, we were really delayed, and as we got closer to New York she came back to ask for something to drink and I could smell the cigarette smoke. I understand the addiction because I used to smoke, but it's not so much that she snuck a cigarette. It's the fact that she lied to me and I didn't know where she put her cigarette. That's our biggest fear, causing a fire. I put on gloves and went through the trash can in the rest room. This is where the glamour comes in. It was really disgusting. I found the butt in the trash can along with nothing but paper.

"We have to serve the food. We turn the ovens on and heat up the food, then place the trays in the cart to pass them out. But passengers can get so impatient. It's not as if we can stand up right after takeoff. We have headsets to pass out, too, if there's a movie, and someone else is passing out the drinks. And in the middle of all of this, there's always a passenger asking, Can I have a pillow? Can I change seats? What about my connection? It's constant questions. And that's why sometimes passing out the food or drinks takes longer. We're constantly getting interrupted. But then that's what we're there for.

"It's easy to feel harried. It's not like you're out of control or anything, but sometimes you wish they'd just give you five minutes. And it's easy to feel unappreciated. I've been talked to horribly. The majority of people I deal with are really very nice, but you always have that handful. You have to realize they're like that to everyone. You just have to keep your sense of humor. It always feels really good to get home.

"At the beginning the travel part was great. I was single and I could go out and have fun in different cities. But as time wore on, that kind of got old. Now I'm married and I have twin daughters. My objective is different now. I could still fly, but right now I want to spend the time with my family. I can go back later maybe.

"Salaries are another downside, though. It's not like it used to be. The older attendants make anywhere from $40,000 to $60,000. But the airline started what they call a B scale for the new hirees. They start off somewhere in the teens.

"Sometimes I sat there and wondered, What are we doing? We're a flying restaurant sailing through the sky with a hundred thousand pounds of fuel under us. Who in her right mind is going to get into this thing?

"But most of the people are really, really wonderful. You'll have someone come up to you and say that's it's been the best flight they ever had, and that makes up for everything."

**Advice from Andrea Gleason**

"I think if you're young and have a lot of energy, it's wonderful. I always joke around and say I'm donning my rhino skin. You need thick skin to do this. I had a flight buddy who teased me and said I'm like Mary Poppins out there. That's what I'm here for. I'm not here to make these people have a miserable trip. I have a hard time saying no to them. It has to be something outlandish. I try not to get bothered by petty things. You're going to see a lot of pettiness, but you can't let it get to you. I had a gentleman who had won a lot of stuffed animals. They were all packed away in the overhead bin. Then another passenger comes in and opens up the bin. All of a sudden he starts throwing all these animals. I looked over and I saw a giraffe flying through the cabin, then an elephant goes and a monkey goes. He thinks it's his bin because it's over his seat. So, sometimes you have to go up and say, 'No, it's *my* bin and I'm sharing it with everyone.' Sometimes you have to treat them as if they're first graders. I know it sounds silly, but I try to give people little life lessons. If someone doesn't say please to me, instead they say, 'Hey, gimme a Coke,' I smile and say, 'What's the magic word?' I do it with a smile. I've been able to say things to people and get away with it, but you have to be able to wear that smile.

"The key to success in this industry is to be extremely flexible. Stuff happens all the time. You get canceled, delayed, diverted, and you have to be able to go with the flow. And you can't be chasing the almighty dollar to work at this job. You have to want just time off and flight benefits. That's really where the fun is. I loved it. Where else could you put in so little time and have such good benefits?"

## FOR MORE INFORMATION

### Hotels, Resorts, Cruises
For information on careers and scholarships in hotel management, contact:

The American Hotel and Motel Association (AH&MA)
Information Center
1201 New York Avenue NW
Washington, DC 20005-3931

For information on educational programs, including correspondence courses, in hotel and restaurant management, write to:

The Educational Institute of AH&MA
P.O. Box 1240
East Lansing, MI 48826

For information on careers in housekeeping management, contact:

National Executive Housekeepers Association, Inc.
1001 Eastwind Drive, Suite 301
Westerville, OH 43081

For information on hospitality careers, as well as how to purchase a directory of colleges and other schools offering programs and courses in hotel and restaurant administration, write to:

Council on Hotel, Restaurant, and Institutional Education
1200 Seventeenth Street NW
Washington, DC 20036-3097

For more information about working for cruise lines, contact:

Cruise Line International Association
500 Fifth Avenue, Suite 1407
New York, NY 10110

**Restaurants**
A guide to careers in restaurants, a list of two- and four-year colleges that have food service programs, and information on scholarships to those programs are available from:

National Restaurant Association
1200 Seventeenth Street NW
Washington, DC 20036-3097

**Travel Agents**
American Society of Travel Agents
1101 King Street
Alexandria, VA 22314

Association of Retail Travel Agents
1745 Jefferson Davis Highway, Suite 300
Arlington, VA 22202

Institute of Certified Travel Agents
148 Linden Street
P.O. Box 56
Wellesley, MA 02181

**Tour Guides**
Do an Internet search or look in the Yellow Pages to find associations for tour guides in the city or at the attraction you're interested in.

**Reservation Clerks and Ticket Agents**
For information about job opportunities as reservation and transportation ticket agents, write the personnel manager of individual transportation companies. Addresses of airlines are available from:

Air Transport Association of America
1301 Pennsylvania Avenue NW, Suite 1100
Washington, DC 20004-1707

**Flight Attendants**
Information about job opportunities at a particular airline and the qualifications required may be obtained by writing to the personnel manager of the company.

For addresses of airline companies and information about job opportunities and salaries, contact:

Future Aviation Professionals of America
4959 Massachusetts Boulevard
Atlanta, GA 30337
800-JET-JOBS

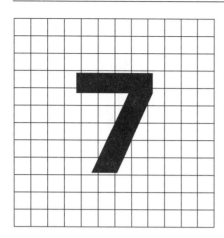

# BUSINESS, INDUSTRY, AND COMMERCE

This is a wide-open field for people who want to use their secondary language skills on the job. Consider these opportunities:

- Multinational corporations such as IBM or Xerox need people who can negotiate and draw up contracts in other languages and deal with foreign clients, making sales presentations here and abroad. They need public relations specialists, lawyers, managers, and executives—all fluent in at least one foreign language.

- Advertising agencies that market their clients' products abroad need employees who speak several languages.

- Book publishers need sales representatives who speak foreign languages so they can more effectively present their foreign language texts to prospective clients.

- These same book publishers may need editors, editorial assistants, copywriters, and proofreaders with foreign language skills. (See Chapter 4 for more information on this area.)

- Computer companies need people to translate software and its documentation into the languages spoken by their international clients.

- Telecommunications companies need workers with foreign language skills to help set up business internationally.

- U.S.-based foreign car manufacturers such as Honda and Toyota need employees fluent in Japanese to deal with design issues, contracts, import/export laws, and sales.

- International bankers and financiers need people fluent in foreign languages to deal with their non-English-speaking customers and clients.

- As an inverse to the above, some U.S. as well as foreign corporations hire people to teach English as a foreign language to local employees overseas. They also might hire teachers to instruct U.S. employees in the local language. (See Chapter 3 for more information on teaching abroad.)

- All of these businesses with international concerns also need secretaries and receptionists and other office personnel fluent in other languages.

Whatever your skill—computers, banking, law, and so on—your secondary language skills can put you on a career track that will utilize your talents and interests to the utmost.

## HOW TO GET STARTED

The need is out there. Once you've identified that need, you can plan your education and training so you can offer yourself as a perfect fit to the company of your choice. Find out what they want, then give them what they want.

Let's look at this possible scenario. A company with export interests in the Persian Gulf desperately needs employees with exceptional sales ability. But equally important is for those employees to be fluent in Arabic and have a strong understanding of and sensitivity to Arab culture. The successful candidate will be familiar with the differences—will know, for example, that to offer the left hand in an embrace or to show the bottom of your shoe would be considered offensive.

People hoping to use a foreign language in their work should spend a year or two—or as much time as possible—in the target country to acquire this specialized cultural knowledge. While the Persian Gulf is not, as a general rule, open to tourists, Egypt and other parts of North Africa where Arabic is spoken are. A stint abroad, ideally staying with a family to learn the complex dynamics of interaction, can add valuable skills to your repertoire.

However, unless you're specifically looking for translating or interpreting positions (covered in Chapter 4), your primary goal will be to acquire the business skills necessary on the job. For example, an undergraduate background in economics, science, finance, and engineering (as well as fluent foreign language skills) would be a great asset when seeking jobs with such automakers as Honda and Toyota.

If you majored in foreign languages, you can still build a case for that degree's application to business, industry, and commerce. There's no doubt that English does dominate business and trade. But your strengths lie in your sensitivity to another culture, and it's these strengths you explain to prospective employers.

## WORKING CONDITIONS

If you targeted companies with overseas interests and landed a job with one of these companies, it is likely that after a time on home turf adjusting to your new job and settling in, you will be offered an assignment overseas. This is the moment you and others like you have been waiting for.

Because every country is different, it's impossible to state emphatically what conditions will be like in your particular area. Ideally, you have already spent time in this region of the world preparing yourself for this eventual assignment, and you know what to expect. The standard of living might be lower than in the United States—or it might even be higher, as it is in some Persian Gulf countries. You might be offered exceptional housing, a transportation allowance, or a company car. The local economy might favor the dollar, and you'll send your children to private school and hire a regular cleaning service or housemaid to take care of your family. Then again, your assignment might be in a brutally hot desert, with political unrest a heartbeat away.

Chances are, the company that hires you will be a large one—small companies don't normally have the budget to send employees overseas on a regular basis. These larger companies have attractive salary and benefits packages, but the competition is stiff and top-notch performance is expected.

## POSSIBLE EMPLOYERS

**Manufacturing Firms**

Manufacturing firms mirror the full scope of the economy; they buy raw materials, they advertise, they sell, they transport, they finance. The products they make—everything from automobiles, computers, and software to plastics and pharmaceuticals—are bought and sold around the world. The need for foreign language speakers is as strong as in any industry.

**Importers**

Importers bring into this country products from other countries. Whether they deal in oil from Saudi Arabia or cut flowers from Central America, importers need foreign language skills to do business with their overseas contacts.

**Financial Institutions**

New stock market centers, increased U.S. investments overseas, and increased foreign investments here at home are creating opportunities for those proficient in a foreign language. No longer is it just the major cities that are involved. Even small-town banks have learned to deal with foreign currencies and exchange rates. The opportunities are plentiful.

**Advertising Firms**

Manufacturers and all sorts of wholesalers, retailers, and others have products and services to offer globally. Whether it's to convince the Swiss to try a new ski boot or to set up an Internet site for L.L. Bean's catalog so people in Japan can understand it and order from it, advertising professionals with strong language skills are sorely needed.

**Public Relations Firms**

Public relations firms not only get the word out, they make sure the word is understood and that it doesn't offend anyone. Those with a foreign language and cultural experiences outside the United States possess the sensitivity this area of business requires.

**Law Firms**

Because of foreign investments and international business, the need for attorneys fluent in foreign languages and expert in international law is more important than ever before. Contracts must be drawn up and interpreted, disputes settled, labor laws and investment practices understood and adhered to, patents and international copyrights filed and protected. Law firms specializing in international law also hire paralegals and legal secretaries and assistants.

**Accountants**

Accountants familiar with international finance and taxation are in high demand. Their foreign language fluency makes them even more marketable.

This is not the full scope of possible employers. Your own research will unearth many more. Other industries, such as travel and tourism, hospitals, and social services, are covered in other chapters in this book.

## FIRSTHAND ACCOUNTS

### Colleen Taber
### Flower Importer

Colleen Taber has been in the cut flower import business for more than twenty years. In the spring of 1994, she became the sole owner of her company, Gardens America. Most flower importers are based in southern Florida, and Colleen's sales office is in Pembroke Pines, near Miami. She also has a warehouse on a runway at Miami International Airport so flowers can go directly from the plane to the cooler.

**Getting Started**

"I started in the business working for my parents, who were the original owners of Gardens America, and learned everything from the ground up. For everything you learn, you can learn two things by your mistakes. So I made sure I made plenty of mistakes. Not by choice, really, just by sheer lack of skill. But what I found is that with the world so competitive, it's much better to have some kind of formal training. We employ three full-time salespeople who sell to three hundred customers and do more than twenty-one million dollars in sales each year. But my sales staff never really had any formal training. Recently, we all enrolled in a Dale Carnegie sales course, and we have seen a big difference."

**What the Work Is Like**

"Most of the flowers that you'll order from a florist shop have not been grown domestically. Although some originate in Europe, in particular in Holland, most are imported to the United States from Central and South America. In general, costs are lower there, land is less expensive, and the climatic conditions are more favorable, saving the expense of heating greenhouses.

"Importers coordinate all the various steps involved in bringing in flowers from growers or suppliers in other countries. We are responsible for the masses of paperwork necessary before the flowers can be shipped to the various wholesalers, brokers, or retail outlets. Some of the documentation includes plant inspections, plant quarantines, and customs.

"Although most importers bring in flowers from a variety of different growers, I work with only one supplier, Gardens of the Andes, which is based in Bogotá, Colombia. I find that if I give all of my attention to the one grower, that's what the grower gives back to me. Because of the relationship with the grower, I can tell them a year in advance what I need them to grow for me, what color varieties I need each week, what I need for a holiday, and I know that their only concern is me. We work so well together that I can send out promotional material to customers and they'll know that on week three, for example, they'll have pompons and alstroemeria in the boxes, on week twenty-two, lilies, fujis, and carnations. There's never a guess.

"Although I work with only one grower, I sell to more than three hundred customers in the United States. I'm unique in the way I work. I'm the only importer who sells strictly on a standing order basis. That means that I call customers or customers call me and say they would like to be a customer of Gardens America. I process their credit application and then I take their order—which is for the same amount every week of the year. So the flowers come in here already sold. Other importers bring in the product and store it in the cooler while they're trying to sell it."

**Advice from Colleen Taber**

"If you want to work as an importer, I suggest you try to get a job with an importer doing whatever you can get hired to do. You can never see a picture as clearly from the top as you can from the bottom.

"Alternatively, find work with a broker who handles all the paperwork that goes to Customs. Or even get a job with U.S. Customs. Then you can see what happens and what all the pitfalls are. You have to be very careful, especially when you're dealing with South America, where there are such strong drug implications. It's a real hardship for legitimate growers, who have to go to extremes to make sure nothing gets into the boxes of flowers except flowers. On this end, every single package is x-rayed and filmed. They even identify the packer; they initial each box. The precautions are very detailed.

"And needless to say, but I'll say it anyway, if you're dealing with growers in Spanish-speaking countries, it's a good idea to know Spanish. The grower I deal with knows English but not all of his staff do, and when someone else answers the phone, I have to know how to communicate with him."

## William Kelvin
## Marketing/Product Manager

William Kelvin has had a long, successful career in marketing. He has been with a capital equipment manufacturer based in North Carolina since 1995. He earned his B.A. in history and Spanish in 1980 and his M.B.A. in 1982 and has been in sales and marketing for more than twenty years.

**Getting Started**

"After I graduated I looked for a job in which I could be involved in activities that would allow me to measure the results of my actions. I wanted to be involved in some sort of free-enterprise business.

"I went to work for a medical supply company as a logistics specialist. Logistics is the movement of materials through distribution to some end point. In the case of the supply company, that would be a hospital customer. I was there two years, and in my second year I was approached to consider going into sales at the same company. I sold a variety of hospital supplies for one year. After one year that company was reorganizing, and I was part of a reduction in their force. In other words, I was fired. I had enjoyed the job, but I did it very poorly. My first foray into it was a disaster. I never asked people to buy anything. I would call on a hospital and show them my products. I'd ask them if they liked the products, if they liked my company, and if they liked me. They'd always answer yes, but I never asked for the order. So getting laid off was not a surprise. I was losing money for them.

"The one attribute I did have was that I had strong relationships with customers. One of my customers was approached by another of her sales reps who worked for a big, well-known company and asked if she knew anyone who might be interested in selling for them in the Baltimore area and overseas. She gave my name, and I was hired. I was with them a total of ten years. The first five years were in sales, and I sold in two different territories, the eastern United States (Baltimore and Pittsburgh) and parts of Latin America. They gave me the training I needed. They told me to ask for the order.

"One of the reasons I was given the Latin America route in addition to Baltimore and Pittsburgh was that I have some working knowledge of Spanish. Not just from my B.A. program—but I spent several months backpacking through South America during summer vacations in college. I didn't want a job that valued my language ability as the primary skill, but I was very happy to be able to use it in a secondary way.

"After five years I was approached by the sales manager and asked if I would consider a job in product management. The rest is history. I had gone through the various stepping-stones in sales—I was a senior sales rep involved with training—and I was also taking some business courses at night. I was being considered for promotion into sales management, which would have been the next step. We had a marketing staff that had very little sales background, very little customer understanding. The sales manager thought I might be interested in moving into marketing to bring a sales perspective to that area. I stayed there for another five years. I started in marketing as an assistant product manager and left as product manager.

"I came to my current company in 1995. The move was prompted by my concern for a failing market in surgical products and the entire acute care business. My new employer was following the health care market into long-term care and home care. I liked being in health care marketing, but I needed to follow the patient."

**What the Work Is Like**   "We manufacture, distribute, and service health care sleeping surfaces. This is more than just hospital beds. For example, there are sleeping surfaces that are used to help heal skin ulcers. The term 'health care' includes long-term care and home care as well as hospitals.

"A lot of people think that marketing and sales are the same thing. A salesman tries to get rid of what he has; a marketer tries to get what he can get rid of. That's a corrupted quote from Ted Levitt, a marketing professor at Harvard. He said it in terms of sales companies versus marketing companies. But what the marketer does is start at the beginning of the cycle and look at the customers and say, 'Gee, I wonder what they need.' Having determined what the market needs, you then take a look at your company and try to determine if this is something you can produce for the customer. Do we know how to produce it, and can we make money doing it?

"At that point we start interfacing with the product development people, who in some industries might be scientists. In my industry, they're engineers. We form a team of people—myself, the vice president of marketing, marketing researchers, engineers, advertisers, a financial advisor, and eventually salespeople—that asks, 'This is something our customers really want; what can we do to meet their needs?' This is the process of idea generation. The ideas might come from talking to the customers, something we saw in a magazine, or just by being out in the marketplace.

"It's a lot of pleading and cajoling and trying to convince others. And when you're trying to find out what the customers need, a whole group of skills revolves around what we call market research. You might set up focus groups, bringing a group of customers together and talking to them, finding out what isn't working in their present environment. That would bubble forth a need.

"After you do that, you want to quantify that need in the marketplace. Maybe thirty people have told you they need a particular device, but I'm not going to build that product for thirty people. I want to make sure there are enough people out there willing to buy such a thing. You do another set of research—this I coordinate with a researcher.

"Concept development is the next step in the process. This is where you develop a word or paragraph that describes the device. You take that to engineers, who will develop a prototype. In our case, they'll make a bed.

"You then take this bed to the marketplace. This is called the alpha site test. It gets shipped to three or four nursing homes or other health care facilities, both here and abroad—I often get on a plane and meet up with it at the end destination. You don't put anybody on this bed; it's not necessarily safe at this point. You just show it to customers—in our case that would most likely be the nurses—and ask them to evaluate it.

"You go into a little circle then of building and taking it out, building and taking it out. Each time you do that, you learn something new. We're trying to improve the product based on the suggestions we get.

"Once you are ninety-five percent sure this is the product you want, you take it to one big final test that's called the beta site test. Here you have a patient use the bed. After you deliver the product, you leave and see if the product will work without you standing there. Later you go back and interview the nurses to see if they are happy with it. The beta site test gives you a go or a no go.

"Concurrently with this you put the bed through other testing—safety checks, for example—to make sure it meets FDA guidelines. We also test for claims. At some point in the future I might want to be able to say, 'If you buy this bed, you will get great healing of skin sores.' I need to be able to document that claim.

"If it's a go, the engineers start figuring out how to mass produce it, and I figure out how we can make money on it. For that I have to look at the cost and how much people are willing to pay for it. One of the big misconceptions in this business is that you take the cost and add something to it. Cost is not determined that way; it's determined by what people are willing to pay. Once I have done that, I take it to the vice president of marketing for approval.

"Then we start making them, and I go into the promotion planning stage. Now that I have a product, I have to find a way of getting the word out. I'll make brochures and do the advertising. This is all part of my job. I also come up with ways to teach salespeople what to say about it. At the same time, I'm crunching a lot of numbers, looking to see how fast the product will be made, how fast we can get it out to the field, how many will be bought, and what our projection is for making money. Once I'm able to set a date for introducing this product, we hold big sales meetings and tell the reps how to sell it, why they should sell it, and set them loose.

"Because we sell to Latin America as well as to the United States, our sales team has to be bilingual. It's a must for good communication.

"I monitor the product to see if it's meeting its sales projections. If I'm not making those numbers, my boss, the vice president of marketing, wants to know why and what I'm going to do about it. If I am making the numbers or doing better, he wants to know why and why I'm not selling more. There's no winning in this business.

"I'm still following up with customers—is the product still meeting their needs, and if not, what changes do we have to make? I also follow up with the salespeople, asking what else they need to sell the product. And with the engineers, I ask whether the price is right and whether we can get the manufacturing cost down.

"I probably put in about fifty hours a week, basically Monday through Friday, eight to six. There's also travel involved, maybe twenty-five percent of my time is traveling.

"I don't choose to make it a stressful job, but it could be stressful for some people, and there are stressful times. If we're introducing a product that's not going well and sales are plummeting and we can't figure out why, it can be very stressful."

### The Upsides and Downsides

"What I like most is the number of different things I get to do. My job is to influence a lot of different people, and the best way to do that is to speak their language. I have to be able to talk accounting to accountants, advertising to advertisers, patient care to nurses, sales techniques to the sales staff, engineering to our engineers, business management to the vice president of my company. No two conversations are alike.

"The biggest downside is that I support people—the salespeople—who are making more money than I am. A lot more money. But for me, marketing is more fun than sales."

### Salaries

"I'm paid a salary and a bonus based on the performance of the products I'm managing. The salary range for people in my type of job is $70,000 to $90,000 a year including the bonus."

### Advice from William Kelvin

"The best marketers have a dual background. They have been salespeople and they also have the formal education—they have an M.B.A. If the company deals with international markets, then a third skill must be the appropriate language.

"My preference is to get an M.B.A. the way I did. After you've been in sales for a while, go back and get it. But the language skills I acquired early on, before I even knew I would need them."

## FOR MORE INFORMATION

The Internet is the easiest and quickest way to conduct research. Fire up your favorite search engine and type in key words for the industry you're interested in. Look for professional associations that can provide information on university programs, career conditions, and job openings. A few are provided for you here.

American Association of Advertising Agencies
666 Third Avenue, 13th Floor
New York, NY 10017

American Bankers Association
1120 Connecticut Avenue NW
Washington, DC 20036

National Association of Manufacturers
1331 Pennsylvania Avenue NW, Suite 1500N
Washington, DC 20004

Sales and Marketing Executives International
458 Statler Office Tower
Cleveland, OH 44115

Software Publishers Association
1730 M Street NW, Suite 700
Washington, DC 20036

Telecommunications Industry Association
2001 Pennsylvania Avenue NW, Suite 800
Washington, DC 20006

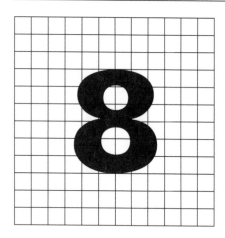

# OTHER JOBS USING LANGUAGE AS A SECONDARY SKILL

Chapters 5, 6, and 7 cover careers that utilize language as a secondary skill. But these are not the only paths you can take to use your foreign language abilities. Here is an overview of other possibilities.

## MUSEUM STUDIES

Art and natural history museums hire multilingual curators, assistants, archaeologists, anthropologists, and other social scientists to work with ancient or foreign texts and negotiate with foreign museums for acquisitions. These positions usually require an advanced degree and serious dedication to the field.

## MEDICAL SERVICES

A foreign language comes in handy for nurses and other medical staff, including hospital administrators, working in ethnic communities in the United States.

Also falling into this category are paramedics and EMTs. They need to be able to speak the languages of their community to provide emergency medical treatment.

Pharmacologists and pharmacists can always use a background in Latin so they can read medical prescriptions.

Pharmaceutical sales representatives who speak a foreign language—French, Dutch, German, Spanish—are often given opportunities to work for multinational companies.

Because of the competition in the United States, some students study medicine overseas the first few years before transferring to a U.S. school. The most commonly studied language is Spanish, a must for students studying overseas.

Some U.S. medical personnel choose to practice medicine or nursing overseas. The Persian Gulf regularly hires American nurses, for example. An understanding of Arabic would be important for communicating with patients.

## SOCIAL SERVICES

State, county, and municipal social service agencies, including welfare offices and immigration, need social workers and staff who can speak the appropriate language for the area and serve clients more efficiently. In various parts of North America, there is a need for workers who speak and understand Chinese, Spanish, French, Haitian Creole, Korean, Vietnamese, and so on.

Police and firefighters need to speak the language of the community to save lives and fight crime more effectively in their districts.

Clergymen in bilingual neighborhoods and missionaries who work overseas need to speak the language or languages of their parish to minister to the needs of their parishioners. Latin and Greek are also helpful in seminary studies.

## MEDIA

While editors and writers need a language as a primary skill, print and broadcast journalists, foreign news correspondents, and news photographers need it as a secondary skill. They write and report in their native language, but languages help them function better in the country to which they're assigned. In addition, they sometimes have opportunities to interview important international figures. Interpreters are usually available, but having good listening skills in the other's language is very useful.

## RESEARCH CAREERS

Source material in a variety of disciplines is often in the original language. University professors and researchers in art and art history, world history, political science, literature, and sociology should be literate in several languages to be able to read material for their courses in the original language, and also to be able to do research in foreign countries. Science professors are often required to learn German to be able to read scientific documents.

Librarians with foreign language reading skills are invaluable for doing research, communicating with foreign libraries, and evaluating books and journals for possible adoption. Local and university libraries, as well as the Library of Congress in Washington, D.C., employ librarians with foreign language skills.

## THE ARTS

Professional classical musicians, such as opera singers and conductors of choirs and orchestras, must be able to read and speak several European languages—Italian, French, German—to understand and preserve the integrity of the text they will interpret.

The entertainment industry—filmmaking, recording, and so on—needs people with foreign language skills to help market products abroad and aid with projects on location.

## ACQUIRING PRIMARY SKILLS

Again, it's important to note that, other than teaching a foreign language, interpreting, or translating, most careers require other skills that are used in the foreground and are considered more important than your language skills. University professors, researchers, and scientists usually have a Ph.D. in their discipline. Medical personnel have M.D.s, R.N.s, and other forms of licensure. Social workers pursue M.S.W.s, musicians hone their craft, and so on. Although an important asset to have, foreign language ability is seen as secondary. Of course, when it comes into play, when the need is there, everyone involved will be impressed and extremely grateful to the linguist who can save the day by communicating in a particular situation. Pursue your career, but by all means, keep your language skills current so they will be there when you need them.

# FIRSTHAND ACCOUNTS

## Maxine Taylor
## Emergency Medical Technician

Maxine has been a firefighter since 1991 and an EMT since 1993. She plans to study to become a paramedic.

**Getting Started**

"My neighbor was the chief of my hometown fire department. As a kid I used to see his truck in the neighborhood, in front of his house, and it fascinated me. He talked to me about the profession, inspired and encouraged me."

**What the Work Is Like**

"EMTs help the paramedics out, making their job easier. We do basic lifesaving, CPR when necessary, apply bandages, get the medications for the paramedics to administer—all the basics. We get a chance to see a lot of things, to be in on everything, because the EMTs go wherever the paramedics go. We get a chance to work with the people, up close and personal.

"We're involved with everything that has to do with saving lives. Calls could be heart attacks, people feeling faint, people having babies, shootings, stabbings, slips and falls, or car accidents. Sometimes we even get called out for minor things, a cut finger or a scratched knee."

**The Upsides and Downsides**

"What I enjoy most is being around people. After the paramedics have done their work and taken the patient to the hospital, as an EMT I get to stay around and talk to the family, explain what we're doing, and reassure them that we have some of the best paramedics in the state, in the nation. We're going to do everything we can to make sure that patient gets better. The patient couldn't be in better hands.

"Because I work in South Florida, there's a large Haitian and Cuban population. I am trying to pick up some Creole, but it's difficult. I am pretty decent in Spanish, though, so that helps a lot.

"The downside is when there's nothing you can do. Where I live we have a lot of swimming pools and, therefore, drownings. The worst part is encountering a little kid who was left unattended and fell into the pool. You do everything you possibly can, but sometimes it's still not enough.

"I try to think about the flip side, that it's always joyful to bring a life into this world when we deliver a new baby and that we save a lot more lives than we lose."

**Advice from Maxine Taylor**

"You need to be the very best at whatever you choose to do, whether it's firefighter, EMT, or paramedic, and remember that hard work and perseverance make everything go well. This advice can go for anyone, really, it's universal. If the mind can perceive it, you can achieve it. If you think big enough, you can do anything."

### Delores Lunceford
### Missionary

Delores Lunceford spent fifteen years, from 1955 to 1970, as a missionary in Seoul, Korea. She worked under the auspices of the Evangelical Alliance Mission in Wheaton, Illinois. She earned her B.A. with a double major in Bible and English at Bob Jones University and her master's in English at the University of Missouri in Kansas City.

**Getting Started**

"Missionaries, like the clergy, feel they have a responsibility to God to serve; I felt this strongly at age fourteen and never lost that conviction. Also, the one thing I was good at in school was language, so I felt confident I could cope with learning and working in a foreign language.

"A college degree was required by the sending organization (TEAM), as well as personal and spiritual qualifications. I studied Greek in college and reviewed it later in a seminary course. I took Latin and Spanish in high school but can read them only with a dictionary. I learned Korean in Seoul from the beginning and continued learning all fifteen years of my life there. I became fluent, but my skills are weakening now, since it's been a long time since I've used the language."

**What the Work Was Like** "When I first arrived, it was a shock to be stared at, to have children line up on the streets to shout, *'Migook saram! Migook saram!'* (American person! American person!). One old lady came up to my husband and clutched the hairs on his arms and yanked; she couldn't believe they were real. This was rural Korea, not the more sophisticated city.

"I was taken by surprise when I arrived in Korea. No histories ever seemed to reflect the realities of postwar Korea. Also, I was dismayed by how complex the language was. I had loved studying Greek and, earlier, Latin, and so was not prepared for the differences in a non-Indo-European language. But I had to start somewhere.

"The rewards of my work were tremendous: changed lives, families rebuilt, suffering comforted. But the day-to-day work often seemed endless and fruitless. It was only as time passed that I could see that good had taken place, that success was in the tiny moments, in the details.

"A woman approached me in the marketplace and said, 'Have you come to tell us about God?' I said yes, so she said, 'Well, tell me.' I was on the spot, and from that day, I stumbled my way through the gospel story almost every day with someone. Sometimes they laughed. I couldn't blame them: the good news that God loves us is almost unbelievable, anyway, and coming with a foreign accent must be even more laughable.

"At first I disliked meeting my language teacher for six hours a day, with no recess, no cafeteria, no schoolhouse, in fact. The first teacher was a lady hired at random (what else could I do?), and she did not speak English. The theory then was that one should not be taught by anyone who knew English. She pushed me gently into a chair, pulled one up for herself, faced me with our knees touching, and spoke forcefully. I had no notion of what she was saying. (Later I realized she was teaching me the alphabet.) She roared into my face, 'KA!' and signaled me to repeat that. So I did, but I guess it was not well done, for she would yell 'KA' at me over and over until I satisfied her. Then followed 'NA,' then 'DA,' and so on, through the whole list. I kept scooting my chair farther back, but she scooted, too, and when we reached a corner, I finally gave up.

"The theory that one should learn like a two-year-old is all very well, but those of us who are not two feel foolish jabbering away without knowing if there is a subject and a verb. So I scrounged in the market and found a grammar book and at night made big charts that I put on the wall to show the way the language hung together. Later, schools were started, and perhaps those students got more help.

"By the end of my term, I loved having a teacher come once a week. We studied the Bible and poetry and idioms and nuances and oh, it was great! But that's the difference between being twenty-two when I started and thirty-seven when I finished. By the end of my term there, I was lecturing in a college and able to associate with more educated Korean people. Also, I was in charge of directing the language study of the new missionaries just arriving.

"Language played an important part in my work—sometimes in totally unexpected ways. My first neighbor eavesdropped on our family. She was hired as my teacher, but in fact, she learned English faster than I learned Korean. This is common because most countries teach English in school and there is a burning desire to learn it. But my sharp-eared neighbor was my first convert, because having learned what a believer's home life is like, she wanted to know more."

**Salaries**

"Missionaries who go out under the direction of a denomination are supported by that group. The great majority of missionaries are independent, though, since more young people want to go than the denominational budget will allow. They go out, as we did, relying on individuals and individual churches that have pledged to send a certain amount each month. There were few luxuries, but we were comfortable."

**Advice from Delores Lunceford**

"I will tell anyone what I was told: the rewards of this work are infinite, but if you are not wholeheartedly committed to being a missionary, it won't work for you.

"Also, if you do not like to study, if you are not enamored of words, of language itself, choose a country with a language closer to English. Spanish and French, for example, are hard enough, but to take on Japanese or Chinese or Arabic, you need to like to study language."

## James Dow
## Cultural Anthropology Professor

James Dow is a professor at Oakland University in Rochester, Minnesota. He teaches Introduction to Cultural Anthropology, Cultures of Mexico and Central America, Ethnographic Methods, Indians of South America, Medical Anthropology, and Mesoamerican Archaeology. He has been teaching in a university setting since 1962. He earned his B.S. in mathematics at MIT in Cambridge, Massachusetts, in 1957, and his Ph.D. in cultural anthropology at Brandeis University in Waltham, Massachusetts, in 1973. He is also fluent in Spanish.

**Getting Started**

"A bachelor's degree in anthropology is not necessary to go on for further study at the doctorate level. I was interested in doing research in a science that was more humanistic than applied mathematics.

"A fellow Ph.D. student who had a job at a local university told me of their search for a new faculty member. I was not satisfied with the working conditions where I was. I was still writing my dissertation and felt that this new university would be a hospitable place to finish it. I was supporting a wife and child at the time and needed a job that would provide income as well as a relaxed atmosphere in which I could finish writing up my field research. The university where I was working before had no interest in advancing the instructors and put a heavy teaching load on them."

**What the Work Is Like**
"A university job in anthropology is very much like an academic job in any other field. The nature of the job depends much more on the university for which you work than on the discipline in which you teach and do research.

"Universities differ in the degree to which they emphasize research versus writing. The few large, old universities may emphasize scholarship as expressed in writing more than anything else. In anthropology this usually takes the form of producing books. At the more numerous, younger universities that do not have a hoary reputation to maintain, the pressure to publish will be much less.

"The most coveted jobs at universities are the ones that lead to tenure. Tenure guarantees people will not be fired for teaching what they feel is right; however, they have to prove the quality of their teaching and scholarship before being granted tenure. This usually takes five or more years. Faculty members usually have to work very hard proving that they can produce scholarship of a quality that gets their work published in good journals. Very innovative and creative ideas are often appreciated by one's peers, but they may not be recognized in the tenure-granting process. Quality teaching is important.

"Before and after tenure, university faculty work very hard. They are usually very dedicated to their jobs. They may concentrate on doing new research, setting up academic programs, supervising student research, or teaching. There is a great opportunity to know students and help them mature personally and intellectually. Many faculty find great rewards in this.

"I usually spend ten or twelve hours a day doing something related to my job. I work as much as I can without jeopardizing my family life or friendships. This means that I usually work at something in the evening or on the weekends. It is often hard to define the boundary between work and leisure.

"Making new friends in a foreign land is a valuable part of cultural anthropology. So is having a foreign language so you can research and read original material and communicate orally with contacts and new friends.

"Many of my hobbies interdigitate with my work. I may be watching television and come across a well-put-together documentary. I may be reading a newsmagazine and find some research that is relevant to my interests. A new computer 'toy' often helps me in my job. My enjoyment of creative photography has been very helpful. I found that my ham radio was also useful when doing fieldwork."

**The Upsides and Downsides**

"The most important thing to me is the freedom to investigate and write about things that are significant to me and, I think, the rest of the human race. I do not have to be beaten down by prevailing political ideologies or narcissistic management philosophies. I can burrow under social, political, and economic systems to see how they work.

"The least pleasant part of my work is the bureaucratic requirements of my job. These do not bother everybody, and many faculty enjoy participating in the bureaucratic structure of the university. The pleasantness of the bureaucracy can vary from university to university. Fortunately, I do not work for a university in which strong management has got the upper hand and treats the faculty like stupid employees. It may sound ridiculous, but there is a tendency in American universities toward 'professional,' rather academically untrained administrators who pay less and less attention to the academic values of the university, and who can make life miserable for everyone. It is important to work for a university in which academic values, which include positive experiences for students, are put first.

"I don't like to give exams and hand out grades. I would like all my students to be fascinated by cultural anthropology and do the best they can, but, alas, they have varied goals and interests. Human nature places limits on the freedom that one can give to students, and therefore the structure of teaching can be a burden at times."

**Salaries**

"One starting out can expect to earn around $30,000 per year. Salaries can go up to $70,000 and into six figures at the most wealthy and prestigious universities. The skills held by most faculty can bring in twice as much in the business world if used competitively."

**Advice from James Dow**

"Check to see what the unemployment level is for the degree you are pursuing. Cultural anthropology can have a rather high level of Ph.D. unemployment.

"Be honest in examining your motives. Ask yourself if you are willing to put up with long years of graduate education, long years of fieldwork, and then long years of job hunting. You will probably have to move to find a job. Cultural anthropologists are expected to enjoy living in foreign countries in rural, underdeveloped areas. Although you may do research in a developed country, you should be excited about living with and studying any sort of human being. You don't have to love them, but you should be willing to live with them."

## FOR MORE INFORMATION

**Museums and Social Sciences**
American Anthropological Association
1703 New Hampshire Avenue NW
Washington, DC 20009

American Association for Museum Volunteers
6307 Hardy Drive
McLean, VA 22101

American Association of Museums
1575 Eye Street, Suite 400
Washington, DC 20005

American Library Association
50 East Huron Street
Chicago, IL 60611

Archaeological Institute of America
675 Commonwealth Avenue
Boston, MA 02215

Museum Reference Center, Office of
    Museum Programs
A&I Building, Room 2235
Smithsonian Institution
Washington, DC 20560

Society for American Archaeology
808 Seventeenth Street NW, Suite 200
Washington, DC 20006-3953

**Medical Services**
American Association of Colleges of
    Osteopathic Medicine
6110 Executive Boulevard, Suite 405
Rockville, MD 20852

American Association of Colleges of Pharmacy
1426 Prince Street
Alexandria, VA 22314

American Pharmaceutical Association
2215 Constitution Avenue NW
Washington, DC 20037-2985

Advocates for Child Psychiatric Nursing
437 Twin Bay Drive
Pensacola, FL 32534

American College of Nurse Midwives
1522 K Street NW, Suite 1000
Washington, DC 20005

American College of Sports Medicine (ACSM)
Member and Chapter Services Department
P.O. Box 1440
Indianapolis, IN 46206

American Health Care Association
1201 L Street NW
Washington, DC 20005-4014

American Medical Association (AMA)
515 North State Street
Chicago, IL 60610

The American Organization of Nurse Executives
840 North Lake Shore Drive
Chicago, IL 60611

American Osteopathic Association
Department of Public Relations
142 East Ontario Street
Chicago, IL 60611

American Psychological Association
750 First Street NE
Washington, DC 20002-4242

American Red Cross
National Headquarters
17th and D Streets NW
Washington, DC 20006

Association for the Care of Children's Health
7910 Woodmont Avenue, Suite 300
Bethesda, MD 20814

Association of American Medical Colleges
Section for Student Services
2450 N Street NW
Washington, DC 20037-1131

Association of Community Health Nursing Educators
c/o 64 Neron Place
New Orleans, LA 70118

Association of Women's Health, Obstetric, and Neonatal Nurses
409 Twelfth Street SW, Suite 300
Washington, DC 20024

Council on Graduate Education for Administration
in Nursing
Duquesne University
630 College Hall
Pittsburgh, PA 15282

Department of Veterans Affairs
Title 38 Employment Division
810 Vermont Avenue NW
Washington, DC 20420

Health Occupations Students of America (HOSA)
6309 North O'Connor Road, Suite 215
LB117
Irving, TX 75039-3510

National Alliance of Nurse Practitioners
325 Pennsylvania Avenue SE
Washington, DC 20003-1100

National Association of Boards of Pharmacy
700 Busse Highway
Park Ridge, IL 60068

National Association of Emergency Medical Technicians
9140 Ward Parkway
Kansas City, MO 64114

National Association of Orthopedic Nurses (NAON)
Box 56, East Holly Avenue
Pitman, NJ 08071

National Nursing Staff Development Organization
437 Twin Bay Drive
Pensacola, FL 32534

Orthopedic Nurse Certification Board (ONCB)
Box 56, East Holly Avenue
Pitman, NJ 08071

Society for Education and Research in Psychiatric/
Mental Health Nursing
437 Twin Bay Drive
Pensacola, FL 32534

**Social Services**
Council on Social Work Education
1600 Duke Street
Alexandria, VA 22314-3421

National Association of Social Workers
750 First Street NE, Suite 700
Washington, DC 20002-4241

National Network for Social Work
    Managers, Inc.
6501 North Federal Highway, Suite 5
Boca Raton, FL 33487


**Media**
American Newspaper Publishers Association
The Newspaper Center
11600 Sunrise Valley Drive
Reston, VA 22091

American Society of Journalists and Authors
1501 Broadway, Suite 302
New York, NY 10036

American Society of Magazine Editors
919 Third Avenue
New York, NY 10022

American Society of Media Photographers
14 Washington Road, Suite 502
Princeton Junction, NJ 08550

American Society of Newspaper Editors
P.O. Box 4090
Reston, VA 22090-1700

Associated Press Broadcasters Association
1825 K Street NW, Suite 710
Washington, DC 20006

Association of American Publishers
71 Fifth Avenue
New York, NY 10010

Association of Authors Representatives (AAR)
10 Astor Place, 3rd Floor
New York, NY 10003

Association of Independent TV Stations
1320 Nineteenth Street NW, Suite 300
Washington, DC 20015

Association of Independent Video and Filmmakers
625 Broadway, 9th Floor
New York, NY 10012

Authors League of America
330 West 42nd Street, 29th Floor
New York, NY 10036

Broadcast Education Association
1771 N Street NW
Washington, DC 20036

The Dow Jones Newspaper Fund
P.O. Box 300
Princeton, NJ 08543-0300

Investigative Reporters and Editors
100 Neff Hall
University of Missouri
Columbia, MO 65211

Magazine Publishers Association
919 Third Avenue, 22nd Floor
New York, NY 10022

National Association of Broadcasters
1771 N Street NW
Washington, DC 20036

National Association of Publisher
   Representatives
399 East 72nd Street, Suite 3F
New York, NY 10021

National Cable Television Association
1724 Massachusetts Avenue NW
Washington, DC 20036

National Conference of Editorial Writers
6223 Executive Boulevard
Rockville, MD 20852

National Newspaper Association
1525 Wilson Boulevard
Arlington, VA 22209

National Press Photographers Association
3200 Cloasdaile Drive, Suite 306
Durham, NC 27705

The Newspaper Guild
8611 Second Avenue
Silver Spring, MD 20910

Producers Guild of America
400 South Beverly Drive, Room 211
Beverly Hills, CA 90212

Radio and Television News Directors Association
1717 K Street NW, Suite 615
Washington, DC 20006

Society of National Association Publications
1150 Connecticut Avenue NW, Suite 1050
Washington, DC 20036

**Research**
Academy of Certified Archivists
600 South Federal Street, Suite 504
Chicago, IL 60605

American Association of Law Libraries
53 West Jackson Boulevard, Suite 940
Chicago, IL 60604

American Library Association (ALA)
Office for Library Personnel Resources
50 East Huron Street
Chicago, IL 60611

American Society for Information Science
8720 Georgia Avenue, Suite 501
Silver Spring, MD 20910

Association for Library and Information Science Education
4101 Lake Boone Trail, Suite 201
Raleigh, NC 27607

Library of Congress
Personnel Office
101 Independence Avenue SE
Washington, DC 20540

Medical Library Association
6 North Michigan Avenue, Suite 300
Chicago, IL 60602

National Archives
Eighth and Constitution Avenue
Washington, DC 20408

National Association of Government Archives and Records Administrators
c/o Director, New York State Archives
10A46 Cultural Education Center
Albany, NY 12230

Society of American Archivists
600 South Federal Street, Suite 504
Chicago, IL 60605

Special Libraries Association
1700 Eighteenth Street NW
Washington, DC 20009

**The Arts**
Academy of Motion Picture Arts and Sciences Academy Foundation
8949 Wilshire Boulevard
Beverly Hills, CA 90211-1972

National Academy of Television Arts and Sciences
111 West 57th Street, Suite 1020
New York, NY 10019

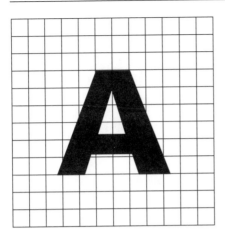

# CONTACT ADDRESSES FOR FOREIGN LANGUAGE JOBS

This is a list of addresses, websites, and contacts for information sources and/or potential employers and internships for language-skilled personnel.

Abbott Associates
801 North Tipp Street
Alexandria, VA, 22314
(Editorial skills)

American Council of Voluntary Agencies for Foreign Service
200 Park Avenue
New York, NY 10003
(Various)

American Foreign Policy Institute
1101 Seventeenth Street NW, Suite 1000
Washington, DC 20036
(Various)

American Translation Association
Accreditation Committee
109 Croton Avenue
Ossining, NY 10562
(Translators)

Defense Intelligence Agency
Washington, DC 20301-6111
(Editorial)

Defense Language Institute
Attn: ATFL-CP
Presidio of Monterey
Foreign Language Center
Monterey, CA 93940
(Language instructors)

Department of Defense
Attn: Civilian Personnel Operations Division, RHR-2
Washington, DC 20301
(Internships)

Department of Defense
National Security Agency
Fort Meade, MD 20755
(Internships)

Department of Defense
International Security Affairs
European and NATO Policy
The Pentagon
Washington, DC 20301
(Internships)

Export-Import Bank of the United States
811 Vermont Avenue NW
Washington, DC 20571
www.exim.gov
(Various)

Foreign Broadcast Information Service
P.O. Box 2604
Washington, DC 20013
(Translators)

House Foreign Affairs Committee
Subcommittee of Europe and the Middle East
B359 Rayburn House Office Building
Washington, DC 20515
(Internships)

International Broadcasting Bureau
Personnel Office
Room 1543, Delegated Examining Unit
330 Independence Avenue SW
Washington, DC 20237
(Various)

Library of Congress
Recruitment and Placement Office
Room G114
Washington, DC 20540
(Translation, research)

Library of Congress
Foreign Affairs Section, Room LM-315
Washington, DC 20540
(Summer intern program)

Marine Resources Co. International
Director of Operations
192 Nickerson, Suite 307
Seattle, WA 98109
(Translation)

Radio Free Europe/Radio Liberty
   Recruitment Office
Oettingenstraat 67
D-8000 Munich 22, FRG
(Translation)

Senate Foreign Relations Committee
SD 446
Subcommittee on European Affairs
Washington, DC 20510
(Internships)

U.S. Department of State
Intern Coordinator
Recruitment Division
2401 E Street NW, Room H518
Washington, DC 20522
(Internships)

University of Iowa
The Translation Lab
W615 Seashore Hall
Iowa City, IA 52242
(Translation)

U.S. Department of Commerce
Soviet and East European Division
Employment Office
Washington, DC 20230
(Economists and business analysts)

U.S. Department of Commerce
Personnel Division
U.S. Census
Washington, DC 20233
(Demographic analysis)

U.S. Department of Commerce
Main Commerce Building
International Trade Administration
Washington, DC 20230
(Internships)

U.S. Department of Commerce
Main Commerce Building
Bureau of East-West Trade
Washington, DC 20230
(Internships)

U.S. Trade Representative
600 Seventeenth Street NW
Washington, DC 20506
(Various)

U.S. Information Agency
Personnel Office, Room 534
400 C Street NW
Washington, DC 20547
(Various)

U.S. Information Agency
Soviet and East European Branch
Office of Research, Room 366
400 C Street NW
Washington, DC 20547
(Summer intern program)

U.S. International Trade Commission
500 E Street SW
Washington, DC 20436
www.usitc.gov
(Various)

Voice of America
Personnel Office
RM 1341, HHS North
330 Independence Avenue SW
Washington, DC 20547
(Speakers)

**Websites**

Bilingual Jobs—www.bilingual-jobs.com

The Federation of International Trade Associations—
www.fita.org/wimain.html

International Information Links—
www.uhs.berkeley.edu/careerlibrary/links/occup.cfm

Languages Abroad.com—www.languagesabroad.com/

The Office of Trade and Economic Analysis—www.ita.doc.gov/tradestats/

U.S. International Trade Statistics—www.census.gov/ftp/pub/foreign-
trade/www/

The Web of Culture—www.webofculture.com

Work Abroad Resources—www.transabroad.com

World Hire Online—www.hire.com

World Trade Organization—www.wto.org

World Wide Employment Office—www.employmentoffice.net

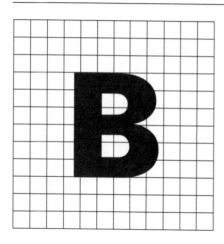

# SELECTED LANGUAGE LEARNING PROGRAMS AND RESOURCES

**International House World Organisation:** International House is a network of 110 schools around the world, all committed to the highest standards in education and business, with the key aim of raising the standards of language teaching everywhere.

International House
106 Piccadilly
London, WIV 9FL
England
www.ihworld.com

For individual Web addresses for the following list, visit www.ncbe.gwu.edu/links/langcult/foreign.htm.

**Directory of Foreign Exchange Programs and Organizations:** Provides an inventory of government and private organizations that administer exchange programs and related educational activities.

**FL-Teach: Foreign Language Teaching Forum:** Specializes in foreign language teaching methods, including school/college articulation, training of student teachers, classroom activities, curriculum, and syllabus design.

**FLAME: Foreign Language Applications and the Multimedia Environment:** Seeks to put foreign language learning in cultural context by using computer-driven multimedia in the classroom.

**Foreign Language and Culture:** Index of links to foreign languages. Site also includes other resource links.

**Foreign Language Testing Database:** This database from National K–12 Foreign Language Resource Center (NFLRC) includes secondary- and college-level tests in languages other than English. The database currently contains more than two hundred tests in sixty languages.

**Foreign Languages for Travelers:** Committed to providing a variety of useful tools for the traveler and those interested in learning a foreign language.

*Hispania*: **Journal of American Association of Teachers of Spanish and Portuguese:** The association's official journal. Focuses on literature, language and linguistics, and pedagogy.

**Human Languages Page:** Comprehensive catalog of language-related Internet resources; database of over 1,300 handpicked links.

**International Language Development:** This website offers free language lessons in French, German, Japanese, Korean, Russian, and Spanish.

**Internet Resources for Language Teachers:** Extensive list of links to discussion groups, language and resource sites.

**Less Commonly Taught Languages (LCTL) Project:** Project's goals are to help advance the teaching and learning of LCTLs by 1) attempting to help LCTL teachers cooperate and communicate and 2) encouraging more people to study less-commonly taught languages.

**Linguistic Funland:** A collection of resources for language, linguistics, and language teaching and learning.

**Multilingual Software Digest:** Comprehensive list of links to websites on world languages and cultures.

**Ñandutí: Early Foreign Language Learning:** This Center for Applied Linguistics (CAL) project offers resources on foreign language learning in grades K–8.

**National Foreign Language Resource Centers (NFLRCs):** There are seven national foreign language resource centers funded by a grant from the U.S. Department of Education to improve and enrich foreign language education nationwide.

**Romance Languages Resource Page:** Designed to bring together a wide variety of texts, news, images, information, and other resources available through the World Wide Web to render them both accessible and useful to teachers and students of Romance languages at the University of Chicago and elsewhere.

**Southern Conference on Language Teaching:** One of five regional affiliates of the American Council on the Teaching of Foreign Languages. For language teachers in the southeast and south-central United States.

**studyabroad.com:** Listings for thousands of study abroad programs in more than one hundred countries throughout the world.

**Technology in the FLES Classroom:** Great site for teachers using computers in teaching foreign languages to young students.

**TPR: Total Physical Response:** Information on the TPR approach to second-language learning and a catalog of TPR books, games, teacher kits, student kits, and video demonstrations.

**University of Sussex Language Centre:** Provides many opportunities for anyone to learn a foreign language either through specially designed courses with expert tutors or by the use of solo-study audio- and videotapes.

**World Language Pages:** These pages point to materials for language learning and make suggestions about how best to use them. Procedural information is also provided.

**WWW Foreign Language Resources:** Aspires to lend starting points for mining the Web for foreign language/culture-specific resources. Seeks to include only the best of the foreign (non-English) language websites out of the many that exist.

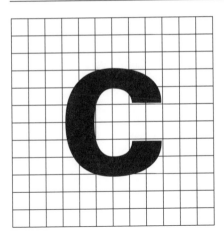

# RECOMMENDED READING

The Modern Language Association (MLA) has an extensive bibliography of important works from as early as 1963 to the present. It's available in print and electronic versions. Learn more about this at www.mla.org/index.htm.

*Guide to Careers in World Affairs* (Foreign Policy Association).

*The Handbook of International Study* (Institute of International Education, 809 United Nations Plaza, New York, NY 10017). For U.S. nationals, this handbook has a section on teaching abroad that contains comprehensive information on opportunities of interest to teachers.

*How to Get a Job with a Cruise Line*, by Mary Fallon Miller (Ticket to Adventure Publishing).

*New Horizons in Education: Pan American's Guide to Schools and Universities Abroad* (Simon & Schuster).

*Schools Abroad* (Porter Sargent, 11 Beacon Street, Boston, MA 02108).

## Books on Careers in Foreign Languages

*Opportunities in Foreign Language Careers*, by Wilga Rivers (VGM Career Books).

*Great Jobs for Foreign Language Majors*, by Julie DeGalan and Stephen Lambert (VGM Career Books).